Chemical Warfare in Colombia

The Costs of Coca Fumigation

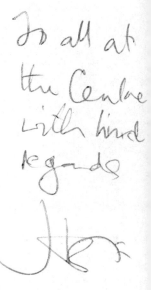

Chemical Warfare in Colombia

The Costs of Coca Fumigation

Hugh O'Shaughnessy and Sue Branford

Latin America Bureau
LONDON

Chemical Warfare in Colombia: the Costs of Coca Fumigation
was first published by
Latin America Bureau
1 Amwell Street
London EC1R 1UL
In 2005

Latin America Bureau is an independent research and
publishing organisation. It works to broaden public
understanding of human rights and social and economic
justice in Latin America and the Caribbean.

Editing: Jean McNeil
Cover design: Diseño Atlántico, Buenos Aires
Interior design and setting: Kate Kirkwood
Printed by Arrowsmith, Bristol
Cover image: shows a mural painted by schoolchildren
in Putumayo, Colombia, with the 'before' and 'after' of
chemical fumigation.
Source: Witness for Peace. www.witnessforpeace.org

ISBN 1 899365 68 0

Contents

Acknowledgements

The authors would like to extend special thanks to Amanda Romero of the American Friends Service Committee for her help during their trips to Colombia to research this book. Dominic Streatfeild's excellent book *Cocaine: an Unauthorised Biography* provided much useful background for chapter two. Andy Higginbottom kindly allowed us to read the relevant sections of his PhD thesis, from which we drew several very helpful ideas. We would also like to extend warm thanks to Jean McNeil at Latin America Bureau and Ralph Smith for their editorial work on this book, and to Tamsin Allen of Bindman & Partners in London for her legal assistance.

Martin Jelsma of the Transnational Institute and Neil Jeffery at the U.S. Office on Colombia read the manuscript and came up with extremely useful suggestions and corrections. All errors that may have crept into the book remain the responsibility of the authors.

1
Putumayo Under Fire

Colombia, the only country in the world to permit the aerial spraying of drug-producing crops, has become the main battlefield in the first chemical war of the twenty-first century. Since the announcement of Plan Colombia in 2000, the Colombian and United States governments have been combating the cultivation of *coca*, the plant from which cocaine is extracted, by drenching the soil of southern Colombia, particularly the *departamento* (department) of Putumayo, with herbicides. The aerial spraying, or *fumigación* (fumigation), as it is known in Colombia, is having a catastrophic impact on the local population and the environment, as will be shown in some detail in this book.

Fumigation is so harmful that it would never be permitted in the European Union or the United States, as government officials have confirmed to the authors. Applied in chaotic and violent Colombia, where large areas of the country lie outside the rule of law, its impact is much more severe, and it is far harder for social movements to show the world what is going on. The Colombian authorities behave in ways that would not be permissible in most other parts of the world: they refuse to divulge the exact chemical formula of the mix of herbicides that is being sprayed, they infringe their own environmental legislation, and they suppress protest.

Despite the social cost, the fumigation policy is not eradicating coca. As is evident from Table 1, peasant families (for whom coca is the only crop that brings a decent income) have responded to the onslaught by planting more of the illicit drug, aware that they will lose part of their crop. This clearly exacerbates the environmental damage by forcing the families to move into new and often more fragile ecosystems, and it means that, unless the authorities are prepared to invest ever more heavily in fumigation, it will fail to permanently reduce coca production. Even though in 2002 and 2003 the amount of coca that survived the heavy fumigation appears to have declined (the figures are, at best, informed guesses), the authorities were denied even this satisfaction in 2004: despite an all-time record in the extent of the area sprayed (136,555 hectares), the amount of coca that survived increased compared with the previous year, albeit by a tiny amount.

Table 1: Coca Cultivation in Colombia 1999–2004 (in hectares)

	Total area cultivated with coca	Fumigated area	Area of coca to survive
1999	165,746	43,246	122,500
2000	183,571	47,371	136,200
2001	254,051	84,251	169,800
2002	267,145	122,695	144,450
2003	246,667	132,817	113,850
2004	250,555	136,555	114,000

Source: Center for International Policy press briefing, March 30, 2005, based on White House Office of National Drug Control Policy, '2004 Coca and Opium poppy Estimates for Colombia and the Andes', March 25, 2005; http://www.whitehousedrugpolicy.gov/news/press05/032505.html

Colombia is not alone in failing to win the 'war on drugs'. Even greater reverses were registered in the UK, where a report leaked to the *Guardian* from the Prime Minister's strategy unit revealed that 'despite interventions at every point in the supply chain, cocaine and heroin consumption has been rising, prices falling and drugs have continued to reach users.'[1] Prices for the two drugs had halved in real terms between 1995 and 2005, reflecting their ready availability. It was estimated that in 2005 there were 250,000 cocaine users in the UK, who spent an average of £5,500 a year each. The total UK cocaine market had a value of some £1.4 billion, with a gram of the narcotic fetching about £60. Crack, at £105 a gram, attracted 140,000 customers in a market worth an additional £1 billion.[2]

The application of poisons in large quantities and in heavy concentrations in Colombia today is reminiscent of Vietnam in the 1960s. Between 1962 and 1971 some 20 million gallons of the herbicide Agent Orange were sprayed on the Vietnamese countryside to remove what the US government called 'unwanted plant life and leaves which otherwise provided cover for enemy forces'.[3] According to the Department of Veterans Affairs (the US federal government body responsible for providing benefits for the 25 million veterans of US wars), there is a 'positive association' between the spraying of Agent Orange and Hodgkin's disease, non-Hodgkin's lymphoma, soft-tissue sarcoma and other potentially lethal illnesses.[4]

Agent Orange (so-called after the orange band that was used to mark the drums in which it was stored) was a mix of two herbicides – 2,4,D and 2,4,5,T – both of which were developed in the 1940s as weedkillers. For years the US public was assured that, although these weedkillers destroyed vegetation, they were harmless to humans. But one of them (2,4,5,T) contained dioxin, and finally, two decades after Agent Orange was applied in such quantities in Vietnam, the Environmental Protection Agency (EPA), the main government body responsible for environmental matters in the United States, admitted that despite 'a large body of research and data collection, there are numerous questions and uncertainties regarding scientific data on and analysis of dioxin risk'.[5] More recently, it has become more explicit, stating baldly that dioxin is 'likely to present a cancer hazard to humans'.[6]

In 2005 came the news that Vietnamese citizens were suing the US chemical companies (including Monsanto) for the health problems they say they have suffered after being poisoned by Agent Orange. In the lawsuit, filed in March, it was alleged that up to four million Vietnamese had suffered persistent respiratory and reproductive problems as a result of the contamination. They are seeking compensation that could run to billions of dollars. Jonathan Moore, a lawyer for the Vietnamese plaintiffs, said: 'The companies...knew Agent Orange contained high levels of dioxin and did not care because...they figured the only people getting sprayed were the enemy.'[7]

Even before the Vietnam War, the US had been given to denying that chemicals useful to the military could be lethally dangerous to local populations. In the immediate post-war years, the military employed DDT (the insecticide dichloro-diphenyltrichloroethane), considered at that time to be a 'miraculous invention', on its bases in the Pacific islands to decontaminate ships and kill malarial mosquitoes in the lagoons. By the late 1950s it was clear that the DDT was doing horrific damage, killing many animals and plants, destroying the coral reefs in the lagoons on some islands, and affecting the health of the local communities. In 1962 scientists finally admitted that the insecticide was entering human and animal food chains and that, as a result, some bird species had been brought to the brink of extinction. However, it took another decade before the EPA banned DDT, and it was only in 1975 that it finally admitted that DDT was a 'potential human cancer agent'.[8]

History is repeating itself in Colombia, where the US is once again denying the damage its chemical weapons are causing. One of the main battlefields in today's war is Putumayo, one of the southernmost departments, on the frontier with Ecuador. Consisting largely of jungle-covered mountains, it is a lightly populated region of the Andes, where hardy coca bushes grow three or four feet high and yield abundant lime-green leaves, from which coca base (*pasta básica*) is extracted. For many years Colombia was not a big coca producer, but imported coca base from neighbouring Bolivia and Peru.[9] It then processed the base into cocaine and sent the finished product to the US and Europe, using speedboats, containers, planes and human carriers known as 'mules'. But in the 1990s the Colombian authorities cracked down on the Cali and Medellín cartels, disrupting the supply lines of coca from the neighbouring countries. The new players – the so-called baby cartels – preferred not to be dependent on imports but to encourage local production of coca, which was easy to do, as the intensification of the armed conflict meant that large areas of the country lay outside the control of the state.

As a result, Colombia became the world's largest coca-producing nation, cultivating three or four times as much as Peru or Bolivia. Within Colombia, Putumayo became the main producing area. By 1999 it was estimated to have just over 58,000 hectares under coca cultivation, out of a total for the country of about 160,000 hectares.[10] Putumayo had more than twice as much coca as the department with the next largest crop (Guaviare, with about 28,000 hectares).

Cocaine production is a two-step process. First the coca leaves – which look very much like common privet – are sprinkled with cement, then pulverised and put to soak for hours in barrels with kerosene and water. The cement, which is alkaline, enables the cocaine alkaloid present in the leaf to be extracted into the kerosene. The kerosene, containing the cocaine alkaloids (which are water-insoluble), separates from the water and the leaves. It is put in a bucket with sulphuric acid into which sodium bicarbonate is slowly added. This causes precipitation, with the release of a kind of scum. When this scum has been dried out, it is known as coca base and contains about 50% cocaine. This fairly simple process is routinely carried out by the peasant families themselves. Coca base is much more potent than the coca leaves – it takes 300–400 kilos of leaves to produce 1 kilo of base – and, unlike the leaves, the base does not readily decompose. This means that, apart from the coca leaves destined for sale in local markets for indigenous use, almost all coca is sold to the middlemen in the form of base. Coca bushes can be harvested three times a year, and each time one hectare of coca yields about 2.2 kilos of base. In a somewhat more complicated and dangerous procedure, some of the middlemen then process this base with more chemicals to produce *cristal*, which is their name for the finished cocaine. They often use household equipment, including washing machines and microwave ovens, to dry out the *cristal*.

The drug production process itself is harmful to the environment. Three prominent Colombians, outspoken critics of US drug policy, have been quick to stress that their disapproval of fumigation does not mean that they deny the extreme harm caused by coca cultivation. In a recent booklet, they pointed out that the relentless expansion of coca cultivation had led to the destruction of much valuable forest: 'The indiscriminate felling of forests causes the loss of biodiversity, not only in the plant world but also as a result of breaking the chains of transformation and the life cycles that link together so many organisms, such as micro-organisms in the soil, birds and insects (which have a pollinating function), reptiles, small mammals and carnivores, among others.'[11]

Their criticisms have been echoed in the United States, where a small group of judges and other members of the public have for some time been calling for the government to set up a Federal Commission to re-examine the government's drug policy. In a recent report, published by the Schaffer Library of Drug Policy, they wrote:

The coca fields are planted along the contours of the land with little terracing and the fields are kept bare of plants except for the coca or poppy plants. These methods, in combination with the steep slopes, serve to strip away topsoil with every strong wind and heavy rain, very quickly making the fields infertile not only for further cultivation but for jungle plant life as well. Recent observers over-flying the jungle describe it as a patchwork quilt of green broken by patches of gray desolation. In addition to causing soil infertility, the topsoil runoff fills waterways and rivers with sediment, changing their courses, causing flooding, and killing fish and aquatic plant life by lowering the oxygen content of the water and smothering the river bottoms. Locals who used to depend on the large fish in the rivers for food, no longer find any fish large enough to eat.[12]

What is driving the expansion of coca cultivation – and is thus ultimately responsible for the damage caused – is the voracious demand for cocaine from the world's rich countries. Even though consumers in the US and Europe pay a lot for their cocaine, peasant families do not receive much of the money. PLANTE (the National Plan for Alternative Development), the Colombian government's agency in charge of the alternative crop programme, calculates that, out of every $1,000 that a buyer spends on cocaine in a rich country, the Colombian peasant cultivating the coca bushes receives only $6. Even so, peasant farmers get a larger income from coca than from any of the other crops they cultivate.

Far from alleviating the damage, official policies are making it worse. Together with the Colombian government the US authorities have declared a pitiless 'war on drugs', which has not only exacerbated the environmental damage, by encouraging peasant families to cultivate more coca to compensate for losses, but has also intensified Colombia's internal conflict by robbing families of their livelihoods and leaving them with little option but join the left-wing guerrillas, particularly the FARC (*Fuerzas Armadas Revolucionarias de Colombia*; Revolutionary Armed Forces of Colombia).

The damage this war is causing in Putumayo is visible to any visitor. One day the guerrillas of the left may be in control of a town or village in the department. The next day it may be the army or their allies, the paramilitary death squads. On some mornings Colombian troops are in great evidence, stopping traffic at roadblocks, but on other mornings they are nowhere to be seen. For days the sky is quiet but then, with no warning, the air hums with the passage of a light spray-plane – escorted by an armed helicopter to fight off possible guerrilla attacks from the ground – flying low to discharge its load of poison. People are always on edge: there are constant casualties in this fast-moving conflict, as the tides of war ebb and flow.

The violence and the suffering were evident to Hugh O'Shaughnessy during visits to Putumayo in June 2001 and August 2003:

'During my first trip, I felt as if I was visiting a war zone. People told me that 134 people had been killed in the town of Puerto Asís alone in 2000 in clashes between the *paracos*, as the paramilitaries are known, and the FARC guerrillas. I travelled along the main road that runs from Puerto Asís, through the oil town of Orito, to the border with Ecuador. It was a scene of wreckage. The asphalt was repeatedly stained with crude oil, which had spilled out from the gashes in the pipeline caused by FARC's bombs. The oil had flowed into the surrounding jungle, polluting the tropical vegetation and casting a dirty film over ponds and watercourses. Every few miles I came across a team, clad in yellow jackets for visibility, sent in by the state oil company, Ecopetrol, to repair the line. Now and then we encountered by the side of the roads the blackened carcasses of heavy lorries hijacked and burnt by the guerrillas. In the fields along the way many crops had been blighted by the aerial spraying, not just coca bushes but also fields of maize and other staple foods. In Orito they told me that 40 people had been killed in 2000 in the fighting.

'Two hours from the Ecuadorean frontier, just north of the Guamuez river, lies the tiny reserve of Santa Rosa, set aside for the 1,300 Kofan Indians who cultivate *yajé*, along with a small amount of coca. A couple sitting on the veranda of their house pointed to lesions on the skin of their undersized little daughter, Franci. She whimpered as her mother lifted her arms to show the boils in her armpits. It was only after Santa Rosa was visited by the spray planes, at Christmas 2000 and again at New Year, that the boils appeared. They seemed to heal over, her parents said, but then they broke out again. In the small-holding behind the house Aurelio, a village elder, showed us stunted pineapples peeping out of their protection of spiked leaves, and the blackened remains of what had once been banana plants. In the fields behind, coca bushes stood dry and lifeless, stripped of their leaves. Farmers in this region know that if a bush can be cleansed of the poison by a good washing within an hour or so of the plane passing over, a hardy plant can survive. Here they had not been treated in time. The fishponds were empty too; the tilapia the villagers bred there for their own consumption and for sale in local markets had been killed by the toxic spray.

'In the little school outside the nearby village of La Hormiga, Gloria, a teacher, told me how early on the mornings of 23 December 2000 and 6 January 2001 planes had time and again swooped low over the playground, flying at the height of a palm tree. "About 230 of the 450 pupils at our school have been ill since then with diarrhoea, respiratory illnesses and constantly recurring skin inflections," she said. The plants the children had been tending in a garden at the side of the playground had withered and all the pullets they had been rearing had died. According to Dr Elsa Nivia, a distinguished agronomist at the nearby town of Mocoa, the local authorities had reported 4,289 cases of skin or gastric disorders among people in the first two months of 2001, while 178,377 animals – mainly fish but also, according to the families, some horses, cattle, pigs, dogs, ducks and hens – had died.

'Food is often in short supply in Putumayo and, at the time

of my visit, hunger was really biting into some villages. The atmosphere was particularly desolate in indigenous communities, which have been struggling for survival since Spanish colonists first came to their lands at the beginning of the sixteenth century and now felt they were finally facing defeat. At a local hospital a doctor talked to me about the daily queues of patients struck down with diseases brought on by the spraying but he begged me not to identify him. He said that the government, his employer, was keen to suppress all accounts of the human cost of the *fumigaciones*, which were presented in Bogotá and Washington as being carefully targeted on coca so that no harm was done to man or beast. Yet often the opposite was true: sometimes while people were talking to me about the damage done to their health and their food crops, I could see rows of healthy-looking coca bushes on the hillsides, stretching as far as the eye could see.

'When I returned in August 2003 the situation had changed. The population was still traumatised by the violence of the previous year: 276 people had been killed in Puerto Asís and 42 in Orito. There were some lifeless coca bushes in the fields, standing beside stunted maize plants and headless palm trees, but at the same time many of the hillsides along the main road exhibited the lime-green shoots of young coca bushes. Either these extremely hardy and resilient plants had survived the powerful herbicide rained on them from the light aircraft, or peasant farmers, for whom coca continued to be by far their most lucrative crop, had planted new seedlings – or both. I also heard reports that some families were planting coca beneath other plants to prevent detection from the air, while others were trying out new strains which might be more resilient to the spraying.

'There were fewer checkpoints manned by soldiers and the road was certainly cleaner than on my first trip. The army and paramilitary offensive had clearly curbed the guerrillas' capacity to blow up the pipeline, and there were no more twisted metal wrecks at the roadside every few hundred metres. The road was eerily deserted. It was obvious from the number of abandoned houses and shacks that many inhabitants had left their villages.

'When I crossed the bridge over the San Miguel river into Ecuador, I realised where some of the people had gone. Though there were no Colombian authorities at the bridge, Ecuadorean troops were out in force. Controls were being rigorously enforced: Colombians had to show their identity cards and an Ecuadorean army sergeant was shouting out from the southern end of the bridge that photocopies would not be accepted. It was clear that the Ecuadorean troops were at the bridge to stem the Colombian exodus. Whereas 362 Colombians had applied to Ecuador for refugee status in 2000, the number had risen to 3,070 in 2001 and to 6,244 in 2002. By August 2003, 5,100 had already begged to be taken in. By then, more than 200,000 Colombians were officially residing in Ecuador.[13]

'Not surprisingly, resentment was boiling up among poor Ecuadoreans along the frontier. Colombia is a much larger, more populous and more sophisticated country than Ecuador. Colombian street hawkers have developed more aggressive selling techniques, and Ecuadoreans were chafing at what they saw as unfair competition. The tension was worst in Nueva Loja, universally known as Lago Agrio (Bitter Lake) because of the pollution caused by the oilfields on which it sits.[14] It is one of the world's untidiest and most unprepossessing towns, somewhere that had clearly been created in a hurry with the cash that had come from the oil boom. On the crowded streets homeless Colombians were hawking their wares more cheaply and aggressively than the locals and were taking trade from them.

'Colombians, too, had cause for complaint. Some of the refugees, especially those who had crossed the border illegally, said they were being harassed and exploited by Ecuadorean employers. The farmers, they said, were not only bossy in the way they treated them – "Look after our cattle, do this and do that" – but they also were refusing to pay them, merely providing food. Some Colombians had considered complaining to the authorities, but were deterred by the prospect of being dumped back over the border into Colombia.

'A few miles from the border post on the San Miguel river, Dr Adolfo Maldonado, a Spanish specialist in tropical diseases, was at work in his clinic in the small town of General Farfán. Colombians were flooding southwards, he said, to escape the spraying. "The fumigations are dangerous and lay the victims open to all sort of damage – genetic mutations, foetal deformities, cancers and miscarriages," he said. A researcher on health and environmental issues with the Ecuadorean group Acción Ecológica, he was examining the women with whom I had travelled on their journey from Colombia over the bridge into Ecuador. They were in General Farfán at his invitation, so that he could check them for symptoms of illnesses brought on by the spraying.

'Maldonado said that it was better for all concerned that these check-ups take place south of the border, away from the influence of the Colombian authorities, which were extremely sensitive to any criticism of their "war on drugs". "We've had little collaboration in our investigations from doctors on the Colombian side," he added. "Many of them owe their jobs to the government and are wary of doing anything that could be seen as critical of official policy." In 2001 Colombians had told a group of non-governmental organisations, which was investigating the effects of spraying in western Putumayo: "We – and people in general – want to talk because it's sad to have to keep quiet. The problem is that whoever talks is killed or has to leave the area."[15]

'On Ecuadorean soil, however, Maldonado is getting results. He has published reports in scientific journals that show that the incidence of illnesses such as conjunctivitis, bacterial and fungal skin infections, acute respiratory diseases, diarrhoea and fevers are high among Ecuadoreans living in border areas affected by herbicide drift. He believes that the spraying may be causing genetic damage. "Blood tests done at a laboratory in the Catholic University of Ecuador in Quito have provided evidence of damage to human chromosomes and DNA chains," he said.

'Maldonado believes that the health of some vulnerable people may have been severely affected by the fumigations, although he admits that it is difficult to prove this conclusively. I watched him at work in his makeshift surgery in Lago Agrio. A young mother, Irene, and her nine-month-old baby, Antony Moreno, were waiting for him. The baby whimpered as his mother stopped breast-feeding so that the doctor could examine his eyes. Irene said she had taken her son with her on a visit to friends on the Ecuadorean bank of the San Miguel river in July 2003, just a few days after spraying had taken place on the Colombian bank. He had developed a galloping infection and had completely lost the sight of his right eye, despite efforts of a surgeon in Quito to save it. Maldonado said it was difficult to be sure what precisely had caused the infection, but experience led him to believe that it could well be the fumigation. Like most Ecuadoreans living in the countryside, Irene and her husband had no health insurance. "We had to get into debt to pay for the medicine and the travel," she said. By the time Maldonado was examining Antony's eyes, the cornea had lost all its colour. Irene had been told that the only solution was a new cornea, which would be cripplingly expensive and almost impossible to get done in Ecuador.

'One young Colombian child, Edwin Javier Daza, was not as lucky as Antony. As recounted by Maldonado, this eleven-month-old old baby was playing in the garden of his home in the Guamuez river valley at 7.30 a.m. on November 15, 2001. An aircraft flew over the house, spraying the land, including a watercourse that the local community used. Edwin was a sturdy child and had previously had no health problems except

for a fever when he was three months old. At about midday
Edwin's eyes went red and he started scratching his face. He
slept for much of the rest of the day, but at 11 p.m. he started
to vomit, had diarrhoea and broke into a cold sweat. His feet
and hands went purple. He cried when he was moved. By the
next morning his whole body had turned purplish, his eyes
were fixed and he was still suffering from diarrhoea. His mother
took him to hospital but he died at 8 p.m. Not a single coca
bush was growing on the small plot of land that his mother
owned. The local doctor could not be sure that the spraying
caused his death, but he could find no other reason for the
rapid progression from normal health to death.'

O'Shaughnessy's experiences raise many questions. What is
going on in Putumayo? What is this poison that the spray
planes are unloading over the Colombian countryside? Why
are the US authorities funding this vicious war on poor
Colombians, particularly as it isn't eradicating coca? Aren't the
authorities just storing up more problems for themselves by
destroying livelihoods and displacing families? Are the US
authorities misguidedly pursuing ill-conceived policies that are
doomed to failure? Or is there a hidden agenda to their 'war on
drugs'? The rest of this book is an attempt to answer these
questions.

Notes

1 The *Guardian*, July 5, 2005, http://image.guardian.co.uk/sys-files/
  Guardian/documents/2005/07/05/Report.pdf
2 Ibid. p. 79.
3 Website of US Department of Veterans Affairs http://www.va.gov/
  healtheligibility/glossary/glossary_popup.asp?word=agent_orange
4 Website of US Department of Veterans Affairs http://www.va.gov/agen-
  torange/docs/IOMIDENTIFIESLEAKWCHRONICLYMLEUKEMIA.doc
5 www.cfan.fda.gov/~lord/dioxinqa.html#gl
6 Quoted in a report to the United States General Accounting Office

(GAO) April 2002, http://www.safealternatives.org/GAOReport.pdf

7   'Vietnam War victims of Agent Orange poisoning sue US chemical companies', *Independent*, March 4, 2005.

8   EPA press release, August 11, 1975.

9   International Crisis Group, *War and Drugs in Colombia*, Latin America Report no. 11, January 27, 2005, p. 4.

10   United Nations Office on Drugs and Crime, *Colombia Coca Survey for 2003*, Bogotá, June 2004.

11   Ricardo Vargas, María Lucía Guardiola, and Jorge Almanza, *Fumigación en Colombia: Los 'Exitos' del Desacierto*, Acción Andina, Bogotá, 2003, p. 7.

12   http://66.249.93.104/search?q=cache:ADybskygmpsJ:www.druglibrary.org/schaffer/cocaine/cocaenv.htm+coca+cultivation+Colombia+contamination+rivers&hl=en&lr=lang_en

13   UN High Commissioner for Refugees and Ecuadorean Foreign Ministry, quoted in Consultoría para los Derechos Humanos y el Desplazamiento, *Plan Colombia: Contraproductos y Crisis Humanitária – Fumigaciones y Desplazamiento en la Frontera con Ecuador*, Bogotá, October 2003.

14   The oilfields themselves were named after Bitter Lake in Texas, where the US oil company Texaco found its first large oil field.

15   Alianza de Fronteras (CINEP–MINGA–CODHES), report (in Spanish) on a workshop on the Lower Putumayo, Puerto Asís, August 27–29, 2001.

2
The US Declares 'War on Drugs'

Although many people today associate Colombia with the longstanding supply of cocaine to the world, the country has been heavily involved in drug trafficking for only 30 years. During that relatively brief period, what was at first a metaphorical 'war on drugs' has been transformed into a very real protracted battle, in which thousands have died as so-called collateral damage. As is so often the case in Latin America, the process has been driven by policies adopted in the United States. In this chapter we will tell the story of how Colombia came to be identified by the US as its prime target in this 'war'.

For several thousand years indigenous communities in the Andes have chewed coca to combat hunger and increase their stamina. Several Spanish and Italian explorers who reached the Americas in the late sixteenth century immediately noted that many Indians had an extraordinary habit. The first written account came from Amerigo Vespucci, an Italian who arrived several years after Christopher Columbus (but nevertheless managed to have the new continent named after him). In a letter to a friend, published in 1504, he wrote:

> They all had their cheeks swollen out with a green herb inside, which they were constantly chewing like beasts, so they could scarcely utter speech: and each one had upon his neck two dried gourds, one of which was full of that herb which they kept in their mouths, and the other full of a white flour that looked like powdered chalk, and from time to time they dipped a small stick,

which they kept moistening in their mouths, into the flour and then put it into their mouths: and this they did very frequently. And marvelling at such a thing, we were unable to comprehend their secret, nor with what object they acted thus.[1]

The Catholic Church was initially horrified by what it saw as a revolting habit promoted by witchdoctors. The First Council of Lima, meeting in 1552, petitioned the King of Spain to ban the practice:

The plant is idolatry and the work of the Devil, and appears to give strength only by a deception of the Evil One; it possesses no virtue but shortens the life of many Indians who at most escape from the forests with ruined life … [It is] a useless object liable to promote the practices and superstitions of the Indians.[2]

However, it was not long before many influential Catholic priests changed their minds, realising that coca brought many benefits to the Spanish rulers (and to the Catholic Church's coffers). In 1609 Padre Blas Valera, a Catholic priest, waxed eloquent about the strange indigenous habit:

The great usefulness and effect of coca for labourers is shown by the fact that the Indians who eat it are stronger and fitter for their work; they are often so satisfied by it they can work all day without eating.… It has another great value, which is [that] the income of the bishops, canons and other priests of the cathedral church of Cuzco is derived from the tithe on the coca leaf, and many Spaniards have grown rich, and still do, on the traffic in this herb.[3]

Somewhat later, European travellers began to examine the coca custom more closely. Dr Clements Markham, in one of many acts by Europeans to draw profit from Latin America, went to South America to procure *cinchona*, the plant from which the valuable drug quinine is extracted. He was amazed at the amount of coca that was produced and consumed. He decided to try it himself and was impressed, commenting in 1862:

I chewed coca, not constantly but very frequently…and beside the agreeable soothing feeling it produced, I found I could endure long abstinences from food with less inconvenience than I should have otherwise felt, and it enabled me to ascend precipitous mountainsides with a feeling of lightness and elasticity, and without losing breath. This latter quality ought to recommend it to members of the Alpine Club and to walking tourists in general.[4]

There is no record of the Alpine Club recommending coca to its members, but other Europeans soon joined Markham's paean of praise. Paolo Mantegazza, an Italian doctor who went to Peru to study the medicinal properties of coca, started experimenting on himself, consuming, it would seem, quite large quantities. In 1859 he wrote:

From 2–4 drachms [6–12 g] one starts to become more and more isolated from the exterior world, and one is plunged into a consciousness of blissful pleasure, feeling oneself animated with overabundant life…I am by nature extremely unsuited to any sort of gymnastic exercise but having reached a dose of 4 drachms [12 g] of coca, I felt myself to be extraordinarily agile and one time I leapt with both feet together onto a high writing desk with so much confidence that I did not even upset the lamp on the table. Other times I felt myself capable of jumping on my neighbours' heads.[5]

It was about this time that an Austrian scientist, Albert Niemann, discovered how to extract the active constituent of coca – cocaine – from the leaves. The method he used – washing the leaves in alcohol to extract the active ingredients, distilling the alcohol solution, mixing it with bicarbonate of soda and then distilling it again to produce white crystals – is basically the method still used today. At the time his discovery attracted little attention because coca and cocaine were assumed to be more or less the same substance.

Coca continued to win enthusiasts. A Corsican chemist, Angelo Mariani, grasped the commercial potential. He mixed coca leaves in wine, which proved to be a good way of extracting the active ingredients, and then sold the fortified wine as Vin Mariani. Sales rocketed. Aficionados included novelist H.G. Wells, US president William McKinley, explorer Ernest Shackleton, Queen Victoria, the inventor of the light bulb and the gramophone, Thomas Edison, and (the fictional) Sherlock Holmes. Believing they had found a problem-free wonder drug, manufacturers in the United States and Europe began to produce further coca-laced products, from throat lozenges to tea. In 1885 a US manufacturer produced a fizzy drink named after its two chief ingredients – coca and kola nuts. Sales of this novel drink soared and eventually led to the foundation of one of the world's largest multinationals.

Cocaine became readily available in pharmacies, and physicians began to prescribe it for a wide range of maladies, particularly for depression and exhaustion. Sigmund Freud began investigating cocaine for its therapeutic qualities and soon became a regular consumer himself. In 1894 he wrote to his wife-to-be in exultant fashion:

> Woe to you, my princess, when I come. I will kiss you quite red and feed you till you are plump. And if you are forward you shall see who is stronger, a little girl who doesn't eat enough or a big strong man with cocaine in his body. In my last serious depression I took cocaine again and a small dose lifted me to the heights in a wonderful fashion. I am just now collecting the literature for a song of praise to the magical substance.[6]

However, the euphoria did not last. Freud, who was a regular user from 1884 to 1896, eventually gave it up, not without a struggle. Though not chemically addictive in the way that nicotine and heroin are, cocaine produces strong psychological cravings. In 1914 the United States and European countries started banning first some cocaine-based products and then cocaine itself, along with most 'recreational' drugs, including opium and marijuana. No one at the time even raised the possibility that unprocessed coca leaves might retain some of the advantages, without the dangers, of the distilled drug.

Richer people began to move away from cocaine, as its perils became known, but by then some working people had started to use it, particularly in the US. Black stevedores in the South, who often had to work 70 hours non-stop, loading and unloading steamboats, had found that cocaine enabled them to work longer on less food. Soon this habit provoked a racist backlash from the better-off white population. In 1901 the *American Pharmaceutical Journal* reported: 'The use of cocaine by Negroes in certain parts of the country is simply appalling. ... The police officers of questionable districts tell us that the habitués are made wild by cocaine, which they have no difficulty at all in obtaining.'[7] In 1903 Colonel Watson, a rabid anti-cocaine campaigner from Georgia, concluded: 'Many of the horrible crimes committed in the Southern States by the coloured people can be traced back directly to the cocaine habit.'[8]

Despite its lingering use among some sectors of the population, cocaine consumption fell heavily throughout the world, and by the early 1930s it had almost disappeared. The decline was the result of various factors: growing public awareness of the dangers, police intervention and the invention of amphetamines, which had the same kind of effect as cocaine but were cheap, legal and apparently safe. However, as one writer has put it, cocaine was 'down...but not out'.[9] South America's cocaine-makers, driven out of legal trade by anti-narcotics legislation, went underground. A new illicit cocaine industry was born, one that was to prove in the long term far harder to control than the old legal one. By the early 1950s cocaine started to come back into fashion, particularly in Cuba, at the time a corrupt and lawless place regarded as an ideal destination by Americans wanting a wild holiday. After the Castro revolution in 1959, cocaine trafficking moved with the Cuban exiles to the US.

In the 1960s drug consumption took off in the US and Europe. The disaffected, affluent students of the post-war generation were keen to experiment with something new and illicit. In these early days cocaine was not the drug of choice. Most opted for the old drugs, such as marijuana, morphine and heroin, and newer discoveries, such as barbiturates. Paradoxically, it was the way that Richard Nixon, who became President in 1969, dealt with the narcotics problem that encouraged many more people to move into cocaine.

Nixon, who coined the term 'war on drugs', knew that a tough anti-narcotics policy would appeal to the 'silent majority' of conservative, white, middle-class Americans who were his electoral base. And he also realised that this 'war' was an opportunity to target poor black Americans, whom he saw as the group most opposed to his administration. The old racist jibes from the turn of the century came back with force. The powerful press magnate, William Randolph Hearst, whose newspapers had introduced the word *marijuana* into English from Mexican slang, started running stories about black men, often carrying knives, who used drugs to corrupt white women.[10] In their book *Whiteout: The CIA, Drugs and the Press*, Alexander Cockburn and Jeffrey St. Clair make it clear that it was Nixon himself who masterminded the racist strategy: 'After a Nixon briefing in 1969, his top aide H.R. Haldeman noted in his diary: "Nixon emphasised that you have to face the fact that the whole problem is really the blacks. The key is to devise a system that recognises that, while not appearing to do so."'[11] Nixon was thus the first US president to use an anti-narcotics programme as a respectable cover behind which he could pursue other goals. As we shall see, it was a strategy that was later applied with brutal effect in Colombia.[12]

Once in office, Nixon pushed ahead energetically with his anti-narcotics/anti-blacks policies. In early 1969, just a few weeks after coming to office, he set up the Presidential Task Force Relating to Narcotics, Marijuana and Dangerous Drugs (which came to be known as Task Force One). In 1973 he created the Drug Enforcement Administration (DEA), which was to become the country's most important anti-narcotics body. According to statistics quoted in the entertaining book *Smoke and Mirrors: The War on Drugs and the Politics of Failure* by Dan Baum, a former reporter for the *Wall Street Journal*, the US federal drug-control budget rose from $65 million in 1969 to $719 million in 1974.

Colombia gets caught in the web

Anxious to stop the heavy influx of marijuana from Mexico, Nixon carried out 'Operation Intercept' in which some 2,000 customs agents were sent to the Mexican border to search vehicles for drugs. Few traffickers were arrested but the operation convinced the Mexican authorities to act more decisively against marijuana cultivation. Although Mexico continued to produce some marijuana (and started to cultivate poppies after the US put pressure on Turkey to curb its production of heroin), the epicentre of marijuana cultivation shifted to the Caribbean coastline of Colombia, especially to the department of Guajira, an isolated and arid region with a history since colonial days of smuggling goods to and from the West Indies. The port cities of Barranquilla, Santa Marta and Riohacha began to experience unprecedented prosperity, but the downside of the drugs boom – which was to become far more pronounced later – was soon in evidence as well. There was a dramatic increase in violence, and the local police force and the judiciary began to disintegrate, eroded by drug-funded corruption.

Alarmed at what was happening, President Julio César Turbay Ayala (1978–82) carried out Colombia's first aerial eradication, spraying thousands of hectares of marijuana with the chemical paraquat.[13] The fumigation was only partially effective and failed to stem the growth of two powerful drug trafficking groups: the Medellín and Cali cartels. They were quick to realise that cocaine offered far greater financial rewards, so in the 1980s they expanded their business into processing coca imported from Bolivia and Peru and trafficking the finished product to the US and Europe.

The genie was out of the bottle, but few at the time were aware of the scale of the tragedy that lay ahead. With hindsight, it is clear that all the elements were present for a massive expansion of drug trafficking in Colombia. The country was conveniently located for access to the US market via hundreds of Caribbean islands, which meant that it was impossible for the US authorities to control all possible trafficking routes. Trafficking networks were easy to set up, as there was a large group of expatriate Colombians living in the US. There were extensive stretches of remote jungle in Colombia, which made it easy to hide laboratories and landing strips. And, more important than all these factors, the country's turbulent history had created a tradition of political violence and lawlessness. The Colombian state did not control vast areas of the country where violent groups were battling for dominance. It was just the sort of chaotic situation in which drug trafficking gangs, attracted by the huge profits, could expand their activities with impunity.

Colombia was born in violence. It was created in 1811 after a protracted and bloody struggle with the Spanish crown, which resulted not in the formation of one large country to be called Greater Colombia, as envisaged by the leader of the independence movement, Simón Bolívar, but in five separate countries: Bolivia, Colombia, Ecuador, Peru and Venezuela. Independence did not change the social structure, so a small elite of white Europeans and their descendants continued to dominate a mass of mixed-blood and indigenous labourers, ranch-hands and peasant farmers. Much of the following century was taken up by struggles for supremacy, either through the ballot box or by force of arms, between two dominant political parties, the Liberals and the Conservatives. Huge areas were marginalised, only to be sucked into the political tussles when violence spilt over into the countryside.

In the 1940s it seemed for a brief period that Colombia might finally start building an effective nation-state. Jorge Eliécer Gaitán, a talented and highly charismatic politician, stood in the presidential elections on a platform of social reform and income redistribution.[14] On 7 February 1948 he led a silent march of about 100,000 people through the streets of the capital, calling for peace and an end to the rule of the 'oligarchs'. A few weeks later, on 9 April, he was murdered in the centre of Bogotá. Until this day no one knows the assassin's motives, but enraged *gaitanistas* went on an 11-day orgy of looting, pillaging and killing. Thus began a nightmare period of blood-letting, known by Colombians as *La Violencia*, which claimed an estimated 200,000 lives over the next five years, a quarter of them in 1950 alone. The methods of murder were often deliberately savage. At the time the Colombian economy was heavily dependent on coffee, and a peculiar feature of the coffee economy exacerbated the conflict: the existence of seasonal coffee-pickers, who travelled from farm to farm during the harvest. It was easy for the various armed gangs to recruit from this large group of rootless labourers.[15]

Order of sorts was restored by a military coup in 1953. After a period of brutal military rule, power was handed back to the two traditional parties, which agreed to stop feuding and share power. This arrangement, which meant that the losing side in elections would nonetheless be given some power, worked until the mid-1980s. Although it gave Colombia the veneer of a functioning democracy, it did nothing to solve the country's deep-seated problem of social exclusion.

By then, left-wing guerrilla groups had emerged, tapping into the widespread social resentment. Even though it is unlikely that these groups could have flourished without this bedrock of profound inequality, the US played its part, making the first of a long series of policy decisions that have fed the violence. Washington regarded Colombia as a key ally during the Cold War, an important front in the drive to stop the Cuban revolution and its sense of Latin American nationalism from spreading into the rest of the continent.[16] The US provided the Colombian armed forces with lavish aid, including funding for a napalm attack on a peasant commune in 1964. Folklore has it that this commune of some 1,000 members was led by an 18-year-old peasant named Manuel Marulanda Vélez. The attack caused outrage, and the survivors founded the FARC, which was to become Colombia's largest guerrilla group (*see* box). Today, Manuel Marulanda Vélez, or *Tirofijo* ('Sureshot'), as he has become known, is the FARC's supreme commander. He has crafted his own form of Marxism– Leninism, which is as peculiar to him as Cuba's version of Communism is to Fidel Castro.

Although the Colombian armed forces had made a mark on the international scene in the 1950s by fighting in the Korean War, they proved incapable of mounting an effective operation against the guerrillas. Their very lack of success gave rise to the formation of the notorious paramilitary groups, and here US military advisers also played a key role. In the late 1960s they recommended the organisation of 'indigenous irregulars' as a fundamental component of the anti-insurgency strategy. As a result, the Colombian authorities enshrined the US Doctrine of National Security in law in 1965, and permitted the authorities to sponsor the formation of paramilitary organisations, which later evolved into AUC (*Grupos de Autodefensas Unidas de Colombia*; United Self-Defence Groups of Colombia). Colombia was thus the first country to set up the kind of private militias that later, again at the instigation of the US, were to wage 'dirty wars' in Central and South America.[17]

From then on, the Colombian armed forces actively sought the involvement of landowners, businessmen and politicians in the formation of these groups, and the country became increasingly embroiled in a bitter civil war, divided into areas controlled on the one hand by the FARC and the smaller ELN (*Ejército de Liberación Nacional*; National Liberation Army) and on the other by the armed forces working closely with the paramilitaries.[18]

The FARC and *Tirofijo*

Manuel Marulanda's authority may have been challenged on rare occasions, but it has never been shaken. His peasant upbringing in the coffee lands of the department of Quindío, where he was born in 1930, shaped his political programme, which can be summed up in the demand that land must be worked for the benefit of the community. The FARC have never been very strong in the cities, and even today it seems to offer little to city dwellers, especially those with a taste for the normal consumer goods of the twenty-first century. In this sense, the FARC are very different from the media-savvy Zapatistas in Mexico, who have expertly publicised their case through a canny use of technology and publicity. FARC's doctrines, insofar as they exist, are vague. They pay respects to the revolutionary experiences of the Soviet Union, Cuba and Vietnam, but say that they are blazing their own trail. FARC attitudes were well reflected in the statement jointly made by Comandante Iván Ríos and Comandante Fernando Caicedo:

We believe that it is from the basis of the principles set out by Marx, without taking them as schemes or formulas or completely fashioned doctrines but as guides...that the model for Colombian reality will have to emerge.... We speak of socialist revolution. If it will be communist or not is a question to be decided later on. The name we will give it is not of the least importance; the most important thing is that we agree that we need a new country.[19]

From the time they were founded, the FARC sought to control territory, and in doing so to amass funds. At first, the FARC did not want to have anything to do with drugs or drug money. When the Medellín Cartel came to the department of Caquetá in 1978 to distribute coca seeds, the FARC forbade farmers from planting the new crop.[20] Within two years, however, the FARC realised that the ban could seriously erode its base of support among the peasantry. They authorised coca and allowed the cartels to buy coca base, provided they

➤

paid a 10–15% tax on each kilogram. Citing the danger of paramilitary infiltration, the FARC gradually took over control of the whole production process, although not the most profitable activities – trafficking, shipping and selling.

In the five departments in the south of Colombia, the FARC are organised into the Bloque Sur, which is made up of 11 fronts. Each front has a certain (variable) number of columns composed of two or more companies. Each company is composed of two groups, each of which in turn has two or more squads, each containing 12 fighters. Although estimates vary, the Bloque Sur is believed to have about 10,000 members.

Women represent 40–50% of the units and, according to FARC statutes, enjoy the same rights as men. In practice, they are forbidden to have relationships outside the FARC, though these are allowed to the men. Lucero, a female guerrilla, joined the FARC when she was 16 years old, leaving her job harvesting coca leaves. At 25 she was commanding a squad. She gave an interesting insight into the appeal of the guerrilla movement for the *guerrilleras* (women fighters):

Most of the girls come from the countryside, and the country girl has very little. She is used to few comforts. When you come here, the movement gives you everything: food, clothing and what we women need – sanitary towels and contraceptives. The girls aren't used to having these things and, in the context of a hard life, it gives us a certain comfort. We don't have to pay for any of it. [21]

Some of the fighters in the Bloque Sur, as in other parts of the country, are under age. According to the US human rights organisation Human Rights Watch, more than 11,000 children fight in Colombia's armed conflicts. While some fight with the right-wing paramilitaries, most are with the guerrillas. Indeed, the FARC have been widely criticised by international organisations for accepting child fighters.

In the 1990s drug money began to overtake kidnapping and extortion as a source of funding for the organisation. Although large sums of money are involved, there is little personal corruption. Drug profits are controlled by the FARC secretariat, for the development of the whole organisation. Even so, the FARC's involvement in the coca trade has damaged its relationship with the local population. Whereas in the past the FARC charged a tax on each kilo of coca base, it decided a few years ago to cut out the middle-man and force farmers to sell directly to it. So the profit that the FARC makes today is the difference between the price it pays to the farmer and the price it can get from the traffickers. The FARC's decision had several unfortunate consequences. It unleashed violence, because the FARC killed middle-men who did not agree to give up trading immediately. It caused severe hardship for thousands of families who had depended on small-scale trading, and opened the way for the FARC to abuse its position by paying the farmers less than the market price. In some regions the FARC, which is not renowned for its rigorous financial management, occasionally ran out of money and failed to pay farmers at all, causing great resentment. Worst of all, perhaps, the new arrangement obliged the FARC to deal directly with the cocaine traffickers, which meant that it became increasingly embroiled in the whole drug business.

In the mid-1990s the guerrillas did their best to take over the autonomously organised *marchas cocaleras*, massive demonstrations launched by a group of peasant leaders – particularly twelve very courageous women – against the aerial spraying of coca fields, which eventually attracted the participation of about 120,000 *cocaleros* (coca growers). Aware of the political possibilities the *marchas* offered them, the FARC started to regiment the process, decreeing, for example, that everyone should participate in them, with only one adult per farm being allowed to stay at home. Tragically for the peasants, the FARC's action led to peasant leaders being branded FARC supporters. Most of the leaders were murdered or forced into exile. Not surprisingly, this put a damper on new attempts by the FARC at popular mobilisation. Today the FARC has lost popular support in almost all regions of the country, due to its use of authoritarian rule, human rights violations and extortion.

The expansion of drug trafficking

Although the internal conflict meant that Colombia was fertile ground for the expansion of drug cultivation and trafficking, there was an additional factor to be stirred into the mix: worsening economic conditions. Throughout the 1970s and 1980s Colombia ranked second in world production of coffee, surpassed only by Brazil. At that time the coffee industry, including processing and transport, accounted for about 8% of Colombia's economic output and generated about half of the country's foreign exchange earnings. Most coffee farms were small, occupying fewer than six hectares of land, and harvesting was a labour-intensive process, because the country's high-quality *arabica* coffee grew on steep terrain. Coffee provided a livelihood for about 300,000 farmers and was responsible for, directly or indirectly, about two million jobs. Prices remained fairly stable because of the International Coffee Agreement (ICA), which provided the framework for the main producing countries to work with the importing countries to keep world supply in line with world demand.

At the end of 1987, however, the importing countries, led by the US, refused to extend the ICA, preferring to let the market set both the quantity and the price of coffee. As a result, world coffee production soared and prices plummeted. Colombia was badly hurt, as its coffee was particularly labour-intensive and expensive. Many small farmers were forced off the land through bad debts. Some of the displaced families moved south and began to cultivate coca. Others moved higher up the Andes, where they started to cultivate poppies, which grow at an altitude of 1,800–3,000 metres, compared with 1,200–1,900 metres for coffee. Between 1990 and 1992 poppy cultivation increased from 1,500 hectares to 19,000 hectares, mainly in the departments of Huila, Tolima and Cauca. This meant that Colombia gained the dubious distinction of becoming the only country in the world to produce all three leading plant-based illegal drugs: cocaine, opium and marijuana.

In the late 1970s crack cocaine was invented in the United States. Until then, all attempts to smoke cocaine had failed. Most cocaine reached the United States in the form of a white powder called cocaine hydrochloride. But it so happens, by a quirk of chemistry, that cocaine hydrochloride is highly sensitive to heat, so when it is burnt it destabilises completely, losing all its mind-altering qualities. According to some accounts, the invention of a form of cocaine that could be smoked was the result of an accident. In the early 1970s, a US cocaine trafficker visited Peru and noticed that some of the men who were working in the laboratory that was producing cocaine hydrochloride were smoking something they called 'base'. The trafficker tried it and was impressed by the sudden rush to the head. Almost certainly, the men were smoking coca base, which, as we have seen, is not pure cocaine but semi-processed coca, which contains many impurities and is the form in which the drug is transported in the Andean countries before being turned into cocaine powder. But the trafficker did not know this. Back in the United States, he and a chemist discovered that by adding a strong alkali to cocaine hydro-chloride, dissolving the result in a solvent and then allowing it to crystallise out, they could quite easily produce a cocaine salt that could be smoked. Because they were 'freeing' the cocaine base from cocaine hydrochloride, they called it 'freebase'. Later people discovered a much more accessible alkali – baking soda. The product that resulted became known as 'crack'. Consumed in this way, cocaine gave the user an immediate, powerful rush. It also turned out to be very addictive. Consumption in the US took off, leading the authorities to launch another massive anti-narcotics initiative.[22]

Reviving the term 'war on drugs', Ronald Reagan, who became president in 1981, spoke of narcotics as the main security threat to the country. Congress passed tougher legislation, which required foreign countries to be 'certified' for their collaboration in counter-narcotics operations. If a country 'failed' the test, it could lose US aid and trade benefits. Not surprisingly, the certification process, by which the US government decided unilaterally whether to 'reward' or 'punish' a foreign country, became highly unpopular in Latin America.

It was Reagan's successor, George Bush Sr (1989–93), who authorised the first big increase in military assistance to Latin America for counter-narcotics operations. The most important element of the new strategy – the Andean Initiative – was approved by Congress in 1989, the year in which the Medellín Cartel reached its apogee. The idea behind this five-year initiative was to concentrate on military and police aid for counter-narcotics during the first couple of years of the plan and then, as the drugs threat receded, to increase the share of the aid that went to economic and social reforms.[23] Under pressure, Colombian anti-narcotics police started to fumigate drugs crops, spraying poppies in the Andes in 1992 and then marijuana in the Sierra Nevada de Santa Marta, further north, in 1993. After a few years, it became clear that the Andean Initiative had failed to reduce drugs cultivation and, predictably enough, the Andean countries never received the substantial economic and social aid that had originally been promised.

The spraying sparked widespread protests, particularly in the Sierra Nevada. People said that the chemicals harmed the health of the local inhabitants, many of whom are indigenous, and damaged the environment in an ecologically fragile part of the Andes. In a booklet published at the time, the Fundación Pro-Sierra, which helped to organise the protests, drew attention to one of the unplanned consequences of the fumigations: the alienation of peasant populations, paving the way for the land to be taken over by left-wing guerrillas and right-wing paramilitaries. The foundation concluded:

> This fumigation has not resulted in the definitive eradication of marijuana. Instead, it has intensified environmental damage,

harmed the health of the human populations and, above all, increased the distance between the peasant sectors and the state, with a significant increase in social discontent. Without realising what it is doing, the state has prepared the way for the arrival in the region of armed groups.[24]

Some families forced off the land by fumigation migrated further south to join the big influx of dispossessed *campesinos* (peasants) into the Amazon region. With virtually no other way of earning their living, many started to plant coca. It is estimated that Colombia's coca plantations doubled between 1995 and 1999, with 95% of the crop being planted in the southern departments of Putumayo, Caquetá and Guaviare, areas increasingly under the control of FARC guerrillas.[25] For some years the Cali and Medellín cartels fought savagely for control of the trafficking networks. While drug-related violence was constantly in the headlines, paramilitary groups, often working closely with the state, took advantage of the smoke-screen to eliminate leaders of social movements and to displace thousands of peasant families, so that more land could be taken over by big farmers. A Jesuit priest, Javier Giraldo, head of the Catholic Church's Justice and Peace Secretariat, published an anguished account of the widespread human rights violations that he encountered on trips he made throughout the country to record such abuses. In the study, provocatively titled *Colombia – This Genocide Democracy*, Father Giraldo wrote:

One fact seemed to me revealing: on 30 January 1993 a car bomb exploded in a street in the centre of Bogotá, killing 20 people. The incident was attributed, no doubt correctly, to the drug cartels and within a few minutes the international press agencies had reported the news throughout the world. In the same month our human rights database registered 134 cases of politically motivated assassinations and 16 cases of politically motivated disappearances. In the case of 26 of the assassinations and six of the disappear-ances, the evidence suggested that state agents had been responsible for the crimes. In another 89 cases of assassination and 10 cases of disappearance, the evidence suggested that the paramilitary groups that work with the authorities had been responsible. This means that, while the drug-trafficking crime that destroyed 20 lives was widely and immediately known throughout the world, the 130 victims of state violence, or para-state violence, were ignored by the global information systems: they did not exist.[26]

Human Rights Watch has recorded the ways in which the armed forces and the paramilitaries coordinated their activities: communication via radios, cellular telephones, and beepers; the sharing of intelligence, including the names of suspected guerrilla collaborators; the sharing of fighters, including active-duty soldiers serving in paramilitary units; the lodging of paramilitary commanders on military bases; the sharing of vehicles, including army trucks used to transport paramilitary fighters; the co-ordination of army roadblocks, so that heavily armed paramilitary fighters could pass; and payments made from paramilitaries to military officers for their support. The most prominent AUC leaders were Carlos Castaño Gil (who disappeared in 2002 and is presumed dead) and Salvatore Mancuso (who demobilised as part of a government initiative in November 2004). Though formally sought by the government, these leaders circulated publicly for many years. They gave interviews to the press and appeared on television. As human rights bodies complained with growing frustration, the authorities made no effort at all to arrest them.

In December 1993 the biggest drug baron of them all – Pablo Escobar, head of the Medellín cartel – was killed by the security forces. This spectacular success did not mean, however, that the government was actually winning the 'war on drugs', as it claimed, but merely that the Cali cartel, which had collaborated with the security forces in Escobar's capture, had won the vicious battle for dominance. With business booming, the Cali cartel decided to bankroll the campaign of the man tipped to win the 1994 presidential elections, Ernesto Samper. Samper was duly elected but, shortly after he took office, evidence emerged of the funding he had received from the cartel.[27]

In 1996 President Clinton stigmatised Colombia as 'the biggest threat to the national security of the United States', branding it an international pariah.[28] The US authorities unleashed a high-level offensive against Samper, even refusing him a visitor's visa. Under pressure, the beleaguered president announced a programme of 'zero tolerance', promising to eradicate all coca plantations within two years. Even though the Cali cartel had reportedly bankrolled his electoral campaign, Samper dismantled it. But once again this did not mean that the authorities succeeded in eradicating drug trafficking: the vacuum left by the disappearance of two big cartels was soon filled by the baby cartels, which in many ways were harder to control than their larger predecessors.

At the same time, Samper undertook a massive fumigation operation, which did not manage to reduce the overall level of coca production but, in a demonstration of the 'balloon effect' (by which squeezing cultivation in one area increases it in another), displaced some coca from Guaiviare and Caquetá further south to Putumayo. Because of the large number of peasant families forced off the land, landowners and para-military groups were able to extend their control of territory. At times, the displaced families, often with FARC support, courageously staged protests. After a particularly intense wave of fumigations in mid-1996, about a quarter of a million *campesinos* blocked roads and occupied land all over the country.[29]

Along with the paramiltaries, the FARC guerrillas benefited greatly from the turmoil. With the government weakened and with thousands of peasant families destitute, the FARC expanded its guerrilla force to 18,000 fighters, becoming the biggest ever guerrilla movement in Latin America. By the end of 1996, it seemed that the US administration's worst fears would be realised: the guerrillas began inflicting serious defeats on the army with a series of surprise attacks on garrisons. By November 1997 a US Defence Intelligence Agency report warned that the FARC could win the war 'unless the country's government regains political legitimacy and its armed forces are drastically restructured'.[30]

This was a turning point. Although the new policy took several years to take effect, it was at this moment that the Pentagon accepted the need for greater military intervention in Colombia, not just to combat drugs but also to defend US strategic interests in the region and to stop the FARC from seizing power. At this period in US history, before the September 11, 2001 attacks, it would have been politically damaging for the Pentagon publicly to admit its planned involvement in counter-insurgency in Colombia. In the wake of the Vietnam debacle, the US Congress had been given far wider powers to monitor US military involvement in such operations. It was thus far easier for the military authorities to claim they were merely taking the 'war on drugs' to the Andes. This was partly true and sounded far more respectable: no opponent in the United States could possibly claim the moral high ground against a government seeking to protect the country's youth from the scourge of drugs. As President Nixon had been the first to discover, the 'war on drugs' was an excellent smoke-screen behind which to pursue far more controversial goals.

Notes

1 Quoted in Dominic Streatfeild, *Cocaine – An Unauthorised Biography*, Thomas Dunne Books, St Martin's Press, New York, 2002, p. 23.
2 Ibid. p. 31.
3 Ibid. p. 35.
4 Ibid. p. 57.
5 Ibid. p. 59.
6 Ibid. p. 70.
7 Ibid. p. 140.
8 Ibid. p. 141.
9 Ibid. p. 174.

10 Sean Blanchard, *How Cannabis was Criminalised*, Independent Drug Monitoring Unit, http://64.233.167.104/search?q=cache:1-www.idmu.co.uk/historical.htm+How+ Cannabis+was+Criminalised&hl =en&lr=lang_en

11 Alexander Cockburn and Jeffrey St. Clair, *Whiteout – The CIA, Drugs and the Press*, Verso, London 1998.

12 Dan Baum, *Smoke and Mirrors: The War on Drugs and the Politics of Failure*, Little, Brown and Co, Boston 1996. Baum believes that the 'war on drugs' continued to be a campaign against black US citizens even after Nixon left office: between 1985 and 1987 no fewer than 99% of those accused of drug-trafficking offences were African Americans. In fact, it was the main reason why detention rates reached such a high rate among male, black Americans: 35% of black men were arrested in 1989 and 44% in 1990. It was during this period that the highly unpopular Vietnam War finally ended and it was widely believed in the US that one of the reasons for the failure of the US forces to crush the Vietcong was the soldiers' heavy reliance on narcotics. As the black population was disproportionately represented among the US troops, this judgement, too, was a veiled form of racism.

13 Maria Clemencia Ramírez Lemus, Kimberly Stanton and John Walsh, 'Colombia: A Vicious Circle of Drugs and War', in Coletta A. Youngers and Eileen Rosin (eds.), *Drugs and Democracy in Latin America – The Impact of US policy*, Lynne Rienner Publishers, Boulder, 2005, p 103.

14 For an account of the factors leading up to *La Violencia*, see Jenny Pearce, *Colombia: Inside the Labyrinth*, Latin America Bureau, London, 1990.

15 Colin Harding, *Colombia – a Guide to the People, Politics and Culture*, In Focus series, Latin America Bureau, 1995, p. 22.

16 Ramírez, Stanton and Walsh, op. cit., p.102.

17 Michael McClintock, *Instruments of Statecraft: U.S. Guerrilla Warfare, Counterinsurgency and Counterterrorism, 1940–90*, Pantheon, New York, 1992.

18 Ramírez, Stanton and Walsh, op. cit., p.102.

19 Quoted in Juan Guillermo Ferro Medina and Graciela Uribe Ramón, *El Orden de la Guerra – Las FARC–EP: Entre la organización y la política*, Centro Editorial Javeriana, Bogotá, 2002.

20 International Crisis Group, *War and Drugs in Colombia*, Latin America Report no.11, 27 January 2005, p.7.

21 *El Orden de la Guerra*, op. cit.

22 Streatfeild, op. cit., pp. 272–82.

23 See Adam Isacson, 'The U.S. Military in the War on Drugs', in

Youngers and Rosin, op. cit., p. 23.

24 Fundación Pro-Sierra Nevada de Santa Marta, *Los cultivos de marihuana en la Sierra Nevada de Santa Marta: una reflexión sobre los métodos de erradicación*, Santa Marta, November 1993, quoted in Martin Jelsma, *Círculo Vicioso: La Guerra Química y Biológica a las Drogas*, Transnational Institute, Amsterdam, March 2001, p.2.

25 Andy Higginbottom, "Globalisation and Human Rights in Colombia: Crimes of the Powerful, Corporate Complicity and the Paramilitary State', unpublished Ph.D thesis, Middlesex University, 2005, p.7.

26 Javier Giraldo, *Colombia: Esta Democracia Genocida*, published on the internet, p. 2.

27 Colombia Journal Online, April 16, 2001, http://66.102.9.104/search?q=cache:RjSWstRwx2OJ:www.colombiajournal.org/colombia59.htm+Ernesto+Samper+funding+drug+cartel&hl=en&lr=lang_en

28 Andy Higginbottom, op. cit., p. 7.

29 Jelsma, op. cit., p. 5.

30 Quoted in Gary Leech, *Killing Peace: Colombia's Conflict and the Failure of U.S. Intervention*, Information Network for the Americas, New York, 2002.

3
Plan Colombia

In January 2000 President Bill Clinton announced Plan Colombia, and in the summer of that year Congress approved $1.3 billion as the initial contribution to the programme, turning Colombia into the third largest recipient of US aid after Israel and Egypt. It was presented as a counter-narcotics programme, which indeed it was, but it was also a broader programme to protect US strategic interests.

It is instructive to spell out precisely what the US military establishment means by 'US strategic interests'. Just after Clinton had announced Plan Colombia, General Peter Pace, a former platoon commander in Vietnam, was appointed Commander-in-Chief of Southern Command (SouthCom), one of the five powerful military commands that coordinate US military activities throughout the world. The smallest of the five, SouthCom is responsible for most of Latin America and the Caribbean and plays a key role in shaping the US administration's policies for the region. At the Congressional hearings to confirm his appointment, General Pace was asked to outline the US's 'vital national interests' in Latin America. This is his answer:

> I see four US interests in this theatre that meet this criteria [sic]. One is continued unhindered access to strategic natural resources in the US SouthCom AOR [area of responsibility]. A common misperception is that the US is completely dependent upon the Middle East for our nation's petroleum needs. However, our largest single supplier of petroleum is actually Venezuela – a country that

provides 15–19% of our imported oil in any given month. Another vital interest is continued stability required for access to markets in the US SouthCom AOR, which is critical to the continued economic expansion and prosperity of the United States. Today our trade within the Americas represents approximately 46% of all US exports, and we expect this percentage to increase in the future. The loss of our Caribbean and Latin American markets would seriously damage the health of the US economy. A third vital interest in this AOR is freedom of navigation, which is critical to our economy and to the strategic movement of some of our naval assets. Of particular concern is continued unencumbered access to the Panama Canal – a strategic choke point and line of communication that, if closed, would have a serious impact on world trade and could create significant challenges for the rapid positioning of our naval forces. Finally, although not technically defined as a vital national interest, I consider shielding our shore from the destructive effects of illicit drug trafficking and other forms of transnational crime a critical concern.[1]

Looking at this statement, it is clear that the Pentagon would consider the violent overthrow of the Colombian state by left-wing guerrillas in Colombia as a very serious threat to all its 'vital national interests'. As early as 1964, just after the formation of the FARC, the US State department had declared as 'one of our principal objectives the elimination of the potential for subversive insurgency inherent in the continued existence of active bandit groups, guerrilla bands and the communist dominated "enclaves" in Colombia's south'.[2] Drug trafficking was not regarded as a threat of the same magnitude. Later in his statement General Pace says:

Illicit drug production and trafficking, and the associated crimes it generates, finances much of the insurgency movement and directly impacts regional stability. Plan Colombia is a significant step in the right direction with long term goals to end the insurgency through a negotiated settlement and defeat the illicit drug industry through eradication, interdiction and alternative crop programs.[3]

Whether deliberately or not, General Pace muddies the water, confusing counter-narcotics with counter-insurgency. 'Fighting drugs' is merged with the idea of 'fighting insurgents'. The Commander-in-Chief makes no mention of the single most important element in Colombia's illicit drug industry: the paramilitary groups. Since the mid-1990s these groups had expanded their drug-related activities, moving into coca-growing areas and tempting peasant families away from the FARC by paying more for their coca base. It was widely acknowledged that the paramilitaries' involvement in the drug trade was much deeper than the FARC's: they operated cocaine laboratories, they smuggled in the chemicals needed for the processing, and they controlled key routes for shipping cocaine out.[4] It is self-evident that any serious counter-narcotics programme must have a strategy for dealing with the paramilitaries. Yet, without quite saying so, General Pace makes it sound as if vanquishing the guerrillas (albeit through 'a negotiated settlement', as had happened in Central America) would simultaneously lead to the dismantling of the illicit drug industry, when this clearly was not the case.

It is difficult to escape the conclusion that SouthCom's most important objective in Colombia at the time was not to combat the drug trade (although that was seen as a welcome by-product) but to neutralise the guerrilla threat. Yet this is something that the Pentagon would have found difficult to admit publicly. There was still public outrage at the horrific human rights abuses that death squads and armies trained and funded by Pentagon had committed in Central America in the 1980s in the war against 'communist insurgents'. Even Myles Frechette, the US ambassador to Colombia (July 1994–November 1997), had warned the US administration of the danger of becoming too deeply involved in counter-insurgency in the country. 'The issue raises too many human rights concerns and has been a searing experience for us in Central America', he wrote in a cable in January 1997.[5] The Pentagon was faced with a similar challenge to the one that confronted President Nixon in his wish to deal harshly with the poor black population without appearing to do so (as discussed in the previous chapter) and, as it happens, it came up with exactly the same answer: the 'war on drugs'.

In fact, even before Plan Colombia was devised, this sub-terfuge was openly proposed by a leading counter-insurgency export, John Waghelstein, who, in an article in *Military Review* in 1987, advocated a 'melding in the American public's mind and in Congress of this connection' (drugs and insurgents) so as to mobilise 'the necessary support to counter the guerrilla/narcotics terrorists in this hemisphere'.[6] Yet before the Pentagon could use the 'war on drugs' to defend the US's 'vital national interests', it had some convincing to do. For the Colombian authorities were proposing a very different counter-narcotics strategy.

The Paramilitaries

The paramilitaries, believed to number about 20,000, began as ad hoc groups of hired guns for both the Cali and Medellín cartels and for landowners who wished to defend themselves from guerrilla attacks and to seize land for growing coca. They are far more loosely organised and much less disciplined than the FARC. Unlike the guerrillas, they have their own turf wars, often fighting between themselves for control of drug networks.

The main paramilitary organisation is the AUC (*Auto-defensas Unidas de Colombia*; the United Self-Defence Forces of Colombia), which brings together many of the main groups. There are, however, a number of smaller groupings, including the ACCU (*Autodefensas Campesinas de Córdoba y Urabá*) who, despite the fact that they are run by landowners rather than peasants, call themselves Peasant Self-Defence Forces.

The structures of the paramilitaries were well described by Luis Carlos Restrepo, President Uribe's Peace Commissioner:

➡

'The *autodefensas* have adopted a federal structure,' he said. 'The military command is officially headed by [Salvatore] Mancuso but, when you learn more about the groups, you realise that regional dynamics count for a lot. For instance, the *Bloque Centauro* on the eastern plains has a great deal of independence, and the *Bloque Central Bolívar* completely disregards the military command structure of the AUC.'[7]

On 15 June 2003 the government signed an agreement with some of the paramilitary groups at Santa Fé de Ralito, under which the latter would cease hostilities against civilians and gather their men in various sites for demobolisation. Five groups accepted the deal: the AUC; the Bloque Central Bolívar, strong in the departments of Putumayo, Nariño and a swathe of land north of Bogotá; the *Bloque Alianza del Oriente*, which operates in the savannah department of Vichada; the *Auto-defensas Magdalena Medio*, one of the groups responsible for the most violence; and *Bloque Catatumbo*, led by Salvatore Mancuso, which operates along the border with Venezuela. Several groups, including *Bloque Elmer Cárdenas*, which is active in the departments of Chocó, Córdoba and Urabá, turned its back on negotiations.

By the end of 2004 about 3,000 paramilitaries had demobilised, including Salvatore Mancuso himself, who is wanted, along with other paramilitary leaders, on drug-trafficking charges in the US. Many human rights activists have expressed concern at the government's failure to set up a mechanism by which the demobilisation process will really result in the complete dismantling of the paramilitary groups. José Miguel Vivanco, Americas director of Human Rights Watch, said: 'There is a real risk that this demobilisation process will leave the underlying structures of these violent groups intact, their legally acquired assets untouched, and their abuses unpunished. As it is currently being conducted, this process does not justify the support of the international community.'[8]

The chequered history of Plan Colombia

Andrés Pastrana was elected President in June 1998, at a time of cautious hope for Colombia. The military offensive by outgoing President Ernesto Samper to beat the FARC guerrillas into submission had failed. The FARC were in control of 40–60% of Colombian territory (depending on whose estimate you accept), dominating the south-west of the country, where most coca was grown. Half of the guerrillas' income, estimated at about $300 million, was said to come from drugs. Many Colombians believed that the only hope of ending the war was through dialogue. The pendulum had swung away from the hard-liners to the peace-mongers. Pastrana won office by offering hope of a negotiated solution to the conflict.

Late in 1998, as he prepared for peace talks with the guerrillas, Pastrana unveiled 'Plan Colombia – Plan for Peace, Prosperity and the Strengthening of the State', describing it as 'a policy of investment in social development, reduction of violence and the construction of peace'. One of its central tenets was the need for large-scale investment in alternative livelihoods for coca growers. Although the plan sounded good, it did not add up to a coherent and convincing strategy for tackling the country's problems. Many at the time saw it as no more than a ploy from Pastrana for getting money. Indeed, European governments, which were initially invited to participate, politely declined, fearing that their cash would disappear into a black hole. At first it seemed as if the plan might suffer the same fate in Washington. President Clinton was courteous to Pastrana as he landed in the US capital on an official visit in October 1998, welcoming his efforts 'to open the doors of dialogue with the insurgent groups', but was cautious in promising aid.

But then the hawks in Washington sprang into action, realising that they could reshape the plan into something that would serve their own ends. Among those lobbying to turn

Pastrana's plan for peace into a Pentagon counter-insurgency strategy was General Barry McCaffrey, whom Clinton had appointed to direct the White House Office of National Drug Control Policy. McCaffrey had previously headed SouthCom. McCaffrey's ideas were fleshed out by Thomas Pickering, a career diplomat who had been important in the crafting of US policies in Central America. Pickering had been US ambassador to El Salvador in the 1980s, when Salvadorean army officers trained by the US had been found to be implicated in – but never punished for – a series of horrific human rights abuses, including the assassination of Archbishop Oscar Romero, the massacre of 900 civilians at El Mozote, and the rape and murder of three US nuns and a lay worker. Pickering went on to become US envoy first to Israel, then to the United Nations and finally to Russia. He was one of a number of architects of US policy in Central America who were later involved in forging policy for Colombia. Others included Assistant Secretary of State Peter Romero and General Charles Wilhelm, former military attaché in the US Embassy in San Salvador.

It did not take long for these new, hard-line views to be expressed publicly, albeit in a somewhat coded fashion. 'We have made clear to all parties that the peace process must not interfere with counter-narcotics cooperation and that any agreement must permit continued expansion of all aspects of this cooperation, including eradication', said Rand Beers, Assistant Secretary of State, Bureau for International Narcotics and Law Enforcement.[9] On 1 November 1999 the US ambassador in Bogotá, Curtis Kamman, who was far more hawkish than his predecessor Myles Frechette, spoke eagerly about the need to put pressure on the warring parties, 'particularly the guerrillas', and argued that the armed forces needed greater war-making potential and 'enough personnel'. General Wilhelm, who had taken over the direction of US Southern Command, called for 'victory on the battlefield'.

The solution to the prickly problem of how to fund counter-insurgency without appearing to do so was to hide behind the façade of counter-narcotics: the US would fund the drugs war in Putumayo and Caquetá, precisely the regions where the FARC were strongest, and it would give Plan Colombia a predominantly military character. A new very different version of Pastrana's plan, in English, was produced in September 1999. The revised plan, with its counter-insurgency focus, was not broadly distributed within Colombia and was passed without discussion in the Colombian Congress. Even before Plan Colombia, US military aid to the country had increased rapidly, rising from $40 million in 1996 to $305 million in 1999. Even so, Plan Colombia represented a dramatic increase, for the US agreed to provide $1.6 billion (later reduced by the US Congress to $1.3 billion) over the two-year period 2000–2001. The whole plan was to take five years to implement.

Completely against the spirit of the original project, the main element of the new Plan Colombia was the formation of three elite, highly mobile counter-narcotics battalions within the Colombian army. They were to be trained by the US army and equipped with 30 Sikorsky Blackhawk helicopters and 33 Huey helicopters, which conveniently meant that a large share of the $600 million allocated for this task went to US arms manufacturers. The battalions were to be deployed in Putumayo and Caquetá. Another sizeable chunk of funds went to the private US contractors, particularly DynCorp and Military Professional Resources Inc. (MPRI – see chapter five), to carry out the aerial fumigation of the coca crops.

The phrasing of the revised plan reinforced myths. The preface stated that drug trafficking had 'leached the resources that the country needed to complete the construction of a modern state',[10] ignoring the fact that the real barriers to nation-building in Colombia were social exclusion, income inequality and violence, problems that had existed for decades, long before drug trafficking plagued the country. The plan also spoke of regaining control over national territory 'to return the sense of security to all Colombians', suggesting erroneously that there was a period in the past when poor Colombians could rely on the state to protect them. Exceeding the limits of its brief, the plan openly endorsed market reforms, stating that banks and state companies, including utility companies and the state-owned mining company, were to be privatised. It seemed clear that neoliberalism was part of the *quid pro quo*, one of the conditions that the US government had demanded for the funding.

The plan paid lip service to social development, dealing in perfunctory fashion with displaced populations, paramilitary groups, alternative crops and peace negotiations. Yet 80% of the funding was destined for the military, and military operations were to be concentrated in the south, where the FARC had their stronghold. Indeed, the target established in the so-called mission statement was to 'establish military control of the south'. The plan admitted that paramilitary violence was a concern: 'Protection of the civilian population requires an increased effort to fight the illegal "self-defence" groups in the drug growing and processing areas', yet it did not present a strategy for achieving this.[11] It was similarly silent on how it would deal with the human rights abuses committed by these groups.

It later emerged that part of the money was earmarked for spending outside Colombia, notably on the construction of four US military bases, known as Forward Operating Locations, at Manta, on the coast of Ecuador, not far from the border with Colombia; Aruba and Curaçao, two of the three Dutch territories off the coast of Venezuela; and at Comalapa in El Salvador. Plan Colombia was also to be used to fund 17 radar sites, mostly in Peru and Colombia, that SouthCom operated. Plan Colombia would thus help the Pentagon to flesh out the new strategy that the Pentagon had developed for Latin America, after it had been forced to scale down its military base in the Panama Canal Zone in 1999, when sovereignty was handed back to the Republic of Panama. Under the new strategy, the Pentagon had moved away from its old practice of having one powerful military base to oversee the whole region, to the idea setting up many more small bases. According to one military analyst, 'this decentralisation is Washington's way of maintaining a broad military foothold, while accommodating region leaders' reluctance to host large US military bases or complexes.'[12]

While the shift in policy could be presented as a reduction in US military presence in the region, it actually enabled the Pentagon to extend its network and to monitor more closely what it saw as suspicious activity in remote areas. Although the US authorities justified the creation of the new bases by claiming that they would primarily be dealing with narcotics, this was not the case. In fact, the US General Accounting Office (GAO) itself concluded that 'adding military surveillance to the nation's interdiction efforts has not made a difference in our ability to reduce the flow of cocaine to our streets.'[13] It is thus probable that the bases were primarily intended to help guarantee US security in the region and to combat left-wing insurgency. As early as 1999 a US State Department official said that 'the new counter-narcotics bases located in Ecuador, Aruba and Curaçao will be strategic points for closely following the steps of the [Colombian] guerrillas.'[14] An Ecuadorean official has also pointed out that it is technically possible for the US troops to be using the electronic capability in their base in Manta, allegedly installed to provide intelligence for counter-narcotics operations, to supply information for Colombia's US-trained counter-insurgency units. Although no one can state with certainty that this is happening, it seems highly probable.

There is no mechanism by which civil society in the host countries can monitor the use made by the Pentagon of these military bases. There are today large numbers of soldiers and contracted employees, reportedly as many as 10,000, deployed by the US military in Latin America and the Caribbean. This is far more people than are employed by US civilian agencies.[15] It acts as a constant reminder of the US's long tradition of military intervention in the region and sends out the message that, if diplomacy fails, the US is in a position to use force to 'solve' disputes.

Two birds, one stone

As Plan Colombia began to be implemented, the US pressed ahead with its insistence that the first priority must be a 'push into southern Colombia'. The idea was to deliver a knockout blow to the FARC and those seen as its allies, while at the same time stepping up the spraying of coca bushes. Two birds would be killed with one stone. The Pentagon contracted a US construction company to build a $12-million Joint Intelligence Centre, equipped with radar, in Las Esquinas in the department of Caquetá. Two more bases operate from Riohacha, the port on the Guajira peninisula in the north, and on the island of San Andrés. The last two form part of the US Air Force's Caribbean Basin Radar Network.

The Centre, which would house US military advisers, the three new Colombian battalions and the mercenaries working for the US private contractors, was well placed for launching counter-narcotics (and counter-insurgency) missions into the main target region of Putumayo, as well as into Caquetá. At the time, the number of US troops permitted by the US Congress to be deployed in Colombia was fixed at 400, along with 400 mercenaries. (In March 2004 Congress, at President George W. Bush's request, increased the limit to 800 troops and 600 mercenaries.)

By the time Plan Colombia arrived, the region had already been through a vicious struggle for control between the FARC and the paramilitaries. In the early 1990s the FARC had been the stronger force, exercising almost unchallenged control in Putumayo. As large numbers of peasant families had moved in, displaced by the violence elsewhere, the region had become an ever more important supplier of coca and thus of funds for the guerrillas, who taxed production. Indeed, Putumayo had become the FARC's most important strategic and financial bulwark.[16] For the paramilitaries it had become a battleground, not just for military domination, but also over who was to control the lucrative narcotics industry.

In 1997 the paramilitaries declared the south of the country to be their military objective. They began by moving into the department of Meta, which lies to the north of Caquetá. As was their practice at the time, they carried out a series of massacres to show that they meant business. On 14 July 1997 two plane-loads of men from the more northerly department of Antioquia, a paramilitary stronghold, arrived in San José del Guaviare and that afternoon set off down the Guaviare river for Mapiripán, a small coca-growing town on the edge of the Amazon region. Two hundred paramilitaries stayed in the town for what a judge later called 'five days of unimaginable terror'. First, they mounted road and river blocks to cut the town off from the outside world. Shouting that they were members of the Autodefensas Campesinas de Urabá y Córdoba, the principal paramilitary group in the north of the country, they scrawled graffiti on many of the buildings. Selecting names from prepared lists, they seized people in their houses and, according to eyewitness accounts, hacked them to death with machetes or decapitated them with chainsaws. Many bodies – some still alive – were thrown into the Guaviare river. Carlos Castaño, a paramilitary leader, later boasted that 'more than 40 FARC members died'. The number of victims was later put at 49.

It was evident at the time that the Colombian armed forces had colluded, because the paramilitaries had arrived at a landing strip run by the army, and the authorities had ignored repeated calls by a local judge for them to intervene. Evidence later emerged that the role of the army had been far deeper. In March 1999 Colombian prosecutors indicted Colonel Lino

Sánchez, chief of operations of the army's 12th Brigade, for planning the massacre with Castaño. On 18 June 2003 the two were sentenced to 40 years' imprisonment. (In fact, by the end of 2003 Castaño had been sentenced by various courts to a total of 102 years' imprisonment; he never spent a day behind bars, however, and is now widely believed to be dead, reportedly killed by rival paramilitary leaders who were unhappy with his repeated criticisms of the AUC's ever deeper involvement in drug trafficking.) The army units that aided the paramilitaries and ignored the calls for help from the local judge were the 7th Brigade and the 2nd Mobile Brigade. The officer in charge was Carlos Eduardo Ávila Beltrán, now a general. Instead of being punished, he was appointed to the comfortable position of military attaché in South Korea. There is also evidence of covert US involvement: shortly before the massacre Colonel Sánchez received 'special training' from the US Army Green Berets on Barrancón Island in the Guaviare river.

In January 1999 the paramilitaries reached Putumayo. Once again, they announced their arrival by committing a savage massacre, killing 26 people and 'disappearing' another 14 in the village of El Tigre near Puerto Asís (widely known in Colombia as Muerto Asís). Capitalising on the fear caused by the massacre, they spread out, village by village. By 2000 the paramilitaries controlled Puerto Asís and maintained regular roadblocks around the town. The municipal official in charge of receiving complaints from citizens told Human Rights Watch that he had collected dozens of reports of forced threats, disappearances and murders carried out by the paramilitaries.[17] He had also gathered testimonial evidence of army and local police collaboration with the paramilitaries. There was further corroborating evidence of who was in charge in the region: peasants said that they had to pay a fee to the paramilitaries for every kilo of coca base they manufactured.

In May 2000 Comandante Yair, a paramilitary leader who had earlier been a member of the Colombian army's Special

Forces and been trained by the elite US Ranger and Navy SEAL units, openly boasted of the close links between the army and the paramilitaries, saying that the AUC was spearheading the military offensive against the FARC in Putumayo.[18] This was merely public confirmation of what everyone in the region knew, for paramilitary forces were moving in ahead of the army and, on their way into new areas, were passing freely through army roadblocks. In October 2000 the FARC launched a counter-offensive, imposing an armed blockade on the main roads and, in protest over government collusion with the paramilitaries, suspended peace talks with President Pastrana. The local inhabitants did not support the FARC initiative (as perhaps they might have done in the past) but appealed to the government for help. Turning a deaf ear to their entreaties, the authorities left the FARC and the paramilitaries to battle it out for several weeks. It was only when the protests began to reverberate throughout Colombia and overseas that the president finally sent in 6,000 troops to quell the violence.

In December 2000 the aerial spraying began. Collaboration between the paramilitaries and the army continued. In March 2001 a local paramilitary leader told a *Boston Globe* journalist that the paramilitaries were moving into areas ahead of the fumigations to drive out the guerrillas so that they could not shoot down the spray planes. He said that it would be virtually impossible for the authorities to implement Plan Colombia without their help.[19] A resident from Puerto Caicedo told a chilling tale: 'The paramilitaries asked around to see who had applauded when guerrillas had criticised Plan Colombia at a public meeting. They then promised to make these same people applaud to the sound of bullets.'[20] These were no empty threats, and the killings continued.

Under Plan Colombia the authorities sought to win the support of the coca growers by offering them a package deal, the so-called *pacto social*. They made a series of guarantees: they would provide each grower with up to 2 million pesos (about £400 or $700) for food; they would develop marketing networks for alternative crops; they would provide the community with technical assistance and help to finance infrastructure projects, such as roads, schools, health posts and electrification; and they would issue formal title deeds for unregistered land. In return, the farmer would agree to change to legal crops, to eradicate all his coca bushes in the year following the payment of the food money, and to plant no more coca. In early 2001 some 28,000 hectares of land were sprayed with herbicide and, with their livelihoods largely destroyed, many peasants signed up to the *pacto*.

The scheme did not work well, however. Undertakings were not honoured, promised sums were not handed over, and the whole exercise was polluted with the chronic corruption that plagues the Colombian public – and indeed the private – sector. In many cases, the commitment to the families not to spray their smallholdings if they signed the *pacto* was broken, and families stood by helplessly as the planes swooped in and drenched their newly planted alternative crops with herbicide. One local official confided:

> Plan Colombia was the worst thing that could have happened to us. There was a lot of corruption as non-governmental organisations from Bogotá invaded Putumayo. We know how to work with people in Putumayo, but with Plan Colombia came a lot of people from other places to manage the projects, and the government only gave money to these organisations.[21]

Disillusioned by the whole process, some families began to accept the food payment while secretly continuing to cultivate patches of coca. This led to angry complaints from the authorities that the peasants were duplicitous.

Even so, Plan Colombia was successful in dramatically reducing coca cultivation in Putumayo. Some observers believe that manual eradication, also funded through Plan Colombia, played a more important role than fumigation in achieving this. Be that as it is may, the area under coca cultivation fell heavily, from 66,022 hectares in August 2000 to 7,559 hectares in December 2003 and 4,386 hectares in December 2004 (see Table 3). The most recent figures may underestimate the real size of the coca area, as farmers have begun to hide coca under conventional crops and deeper in the forest to avoid detection, but it is clear that in the early years the decline was marked.

Although the spraying was heaviest in Putumayo, it also occurred in other regions. The devastation led to protests by thousands of peasant families. Under pressure from the local communities, the governors of the six affected departments lobbied central government to switch from spraying to manual eradication. The government refused but agreed to improve co-ordination: in the future, PLANTE, the government body in charge of the alternative crop programme, would inform the anti-narcotics department of the location of farmers who had signed *pactos*.

In December 2001 the US Congress approved an additional $625 million in counter-narcotics aid as part of the Bush administration's Andean Regional Initiative. Some of the cash was to go to Peru, where $27 million was to be spent on drug interdiction, compared with a mere $5 million on alternative development. Another $20 million was destined for Ecuador, where again the lion's share ($12 million) was to go on inter-diction, compared with $8 million on alternative development. Only in Bolivia was alternative development to get the larger slice of the pie ($85 million, compared with $25 million on interdiction). For good measure, $18 million was set aside for Brazil and Panama.

In June 2002 the US strategy received a big boost with the victory of Alvaro Uribe in the presidential elections. Colombians had tired of President Pastrana's vacillating policies and his failure to deliver the peace he had promised and, in another swing of the Colombian political pendulum, had opted for a hard-liner. Uribe, who has developed a strategy of so-called 'democratic security' and, as this book went to press, was trying to change the constitution so that he could stand for re-election in 2006, has been extremely tough: he has suspended civil liberties and increased military powers in areas of strategic importance (initially in some of the departments hosting the Caño Limón oil pipeline, which runs from Arauca to the Caribbean coast); he has recruited 15,000 'peasant soldiers' to help in the war against the guerrillas; he has built up a network of civilian informers, which he hopes will eventually be one million strong (and is similar to President Bush's mooted Terrorism, Information and Preventions System, TIPS, a scheme for recruiting one million postmen, plumbers, electricians and so on in the 'fight against terrorism', which was voted down by Congress in November 2002); and he has carried out peace negotiations with some of the main paramilitary forces, which so far has permitted 3,000 paramilitaries to disband, without any of them being properly punished for human rights abuses.

To be more effective in the battle with the guerrillas, Uribe has greatly increased the number of combat troops. Anxious not to change the military draft raft laws, which favour the middle classes by permitting those who have completed secondary school to avoid conscription, Uribe has had to increase compulsory military service from 18 months to two years. As one commentator has pointed out, 'Uribe's expansion of the armed forces has meant an increased recruitment of Colombia's poor, who already constituted a large majority of the three principal armed groups: the armed forces, the paramilitaries and the guerrillas. In other words, increasing numbers of poor continue to kill each other as the government seeks to protect a political, social and economic system that benefits a small wealthy elite.'[22]

Plan Colombia: has it worked?

The US and Colombian authorities have repeatedly proclaimed the success of Plan Colombia in its stated objective of reducing the production of drugs. Indeed, figures from the United Nations (which differ quite substantially from those from the White House quoted in chapter one) show that coca cultivation in Colombia fell from an all-time high of 163,000 hectares in December 2000 to 80,000 hectares in December 2004 (see Figure 1). Even so, despite the marked decline, Colombia is still producing more coca than any other country, with the area under coca cultivation higher in 2004 than in 1997 (when it covered 79,000 hectares).

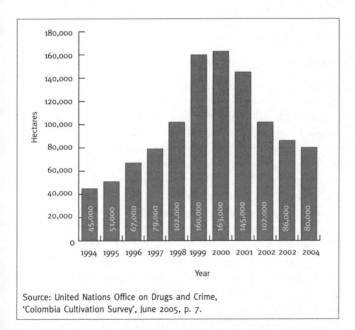

Source: United Nations Office on Drugs and Crime, 'Colombia Cultivation Survey', June 2005, p. 7.

Figure 1: Coca Cultivation in Colombia, 1984–2004

Table 2: Coca cultivation by department in Colombia, 2000–2004 (in hectares)

Department	Aug 2000	Nov 2001	Dec 2002	Dec 2003	Dec 2004	% of 2004 total
Meta	11,123	11,425	9,222	12,814	18,740	23%
Nariño	9,343	7,494	15,131	17,628	14,154	18%
Guaviare	17,619	25,553	27,381	16,163	9,769	12%
Caquetá	26,603	14,516	8,412	7,230	6,500	8%
Antioquia	2,547	3,171	3,030	4,273	5,168	6%
Vichada	4,935	9,166	4,910	3,818	4,692	6%
Putumayo	66,022	47,120	13,725	7,559	4,386	5%
Others	24,318	26,362	20,260	16,855	16,941	22%
Total	162,510	144,807	102,071	86,340	80,350	
Rounded total	163,000	145,000	102,000	86,000	80,000	

Source: United Nations Office on Drugs and Crime, 'Colombia Cultivation Survey', June 2005, p. 15.

However, the reduction, of more than 50% in four years, which is certainly impressive, was achieved in ways that call into question the long-term viability of the strategy (which, as we have seen, was largely concocted in Washington). First of all, the steep declines in Putumayo, Caquetá and Guaviare have been accompanied by increases, albeit smaller, in Meta, Nariño (until 2004) and Antioquia (*see* Table 2). In other words, peasant families have moved elsewhere to avoid the fumigations. This has also happened at a national level, with coca cultivation increasing in both Bolivia and Peru in 2004 so that, despite the heavy fumigation in Colombia, the area planted with coca in the Andean region as a whole actually increased from 2003 to 2004 (see Figure 2). Second – and even more important – the heavy decline in coca cultivation in Colombia was achieved only through massive spraying with

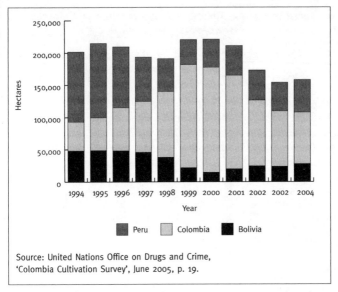

Source: United Nations Office on Drugs and Crime,
'Colombia Cultivation Survey', June 2005, p. 19.

Figure 2: Coca Cultivation in the Andean Region

herbicides (see Figure 3). In all, 136,551 hectares of coca were
sprayed in 2004. If we assume that the spraying managed to
kill most of the crop, this suggests that in 2004 at least 200,000
hectares of land were planted with coca, an all-time record.

The implications are not lost on drug experts. In October
2004 a top Colombian drug adviser, Alberto Rueda, resigned in
protest over the government's failure to modify its counter-
narcotics strategy, making public his letter of resignation. 'Mr.
President.' the missive begins,

> I have decided to make the document I sent you on October 19
> into an open letter asking for a true course change away from the
> current anti-drug policy.... Colombia may be devoting all of its
> efforts against this scourge [of drugs], but it is an effort in the
> wrong direction, incomplete and without hope of ending this
> agony anytime soon.... The emphasis on zero tolerance and

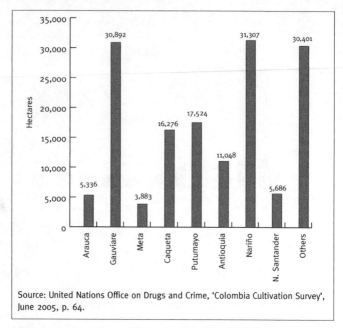

Source: United Nations Office on Drugs and Crime, 'Colombia Cultivation Survey', June 2005, p. 64.

Figure 3: Spraying of Coca Cultivation in Colombia, 2004,

fighting – mainly militarily – against supply has diverted us from a balanced vision, one requiring equal results in demand-reduction and a full understanding of the shared responsibility between drug-consuming and producing countries.[23]

He pointed out that, even though a huge area of land – 132,817 hectares, more than ever before – had been sprayed with herbicides in 2003, it had led to a reduction of only 15,731 hectares of cultivation. This eradication worked out at the huge outlay of $5,243 per hectare. It would have been far better, he said, if this money had been spent on promoting alternative crops. Government figures suggest that the absurdity became even clearer in 2004, when, despite even heavier spraying, the area under coca declined by only 6,000 hectares, according to the UN figures (and actually increased, according to the White House figures quoted in chapter one).

Moreover, it is clear that the reduction in coca cultivation achieved in 2004 will be maintained only if the authorities are prepared to continue heavy fumigation – which is difficult to sustain, from a political, social, financial or environmental point of view. Some observers in the US are beginning to recognize this. In a report issued in 2003, the US General Accounting Office (GAO) observed: 'Neither the Colombian Army nor the Colombian National Police can sustain ongoing counter-narcotics programs without continued U.S. funding and contractor support for the foreseeable future.'[24] Some members of Congress are becoming reluctant to underwrite indefinitely an expensive drugs war in Colombia, given the heavy demand on their resources in other theatres in the 'global war on terrorism' and at home in the reconstruction following the 2005 hurricanes. Even so, it seems likely that the Bush administration will secure approval for an extension of Plan Colombia when it expires in December 2005. The US State Department has said that it will be asking for $731 million in fiscal 2006.

Despite the setbacks, both governments announced their intention of gritting their teeth and continuing with the spraying. When Condoleezza Rice, the US Secretary of State, visited Bogotá on 27 April 2005 she declared at a press conference at the US embassy that 'Plan Colombia has been very successful'. In August 2005 President Bush invited President Uribe and his wife to spend a few days with him and Mrs Bush on their Texan ranch – a sure sign of presidential approval. At a press conference, Bush praised Uribe's policies, saying that 'this is the way to promote security and democracy in the Americas'. Uribe replied in similar fashion, saying that 'the great enemy of Colombian democracy is terrorism. And our great partner in defeating terrorism has been the government and the people of the United States.'[25]

Moreover, to judge Plan Colombia merely by its success in combating drugs is to fall into the trap created by the official rhetoric: the main objective of Plan Colombia was not to eradicate drugs (although the US government also hoped to reduce the supply of cocaine into the United States) but to fight the guerrillas. Only this can explain why Plan Colombia has done so little to target the paramilitaries and the drug-trafficking networks. Since the events of 11 September 2001, the US authorities have been far less coy about admitting to their real goals. Although it may sound tactless to say so, the terrorist attacks in New York and Washington afforded some relief to Colombia policy-makers in the US. The FARC and ELN guerrillas, who had been branded 'communists' during the Cold War and turned into 'narco-guerrillas' during the 'war on drugs', could now be openly attacked as 'terrorists' who threatened US long-term economic and geopolitical interests, which is what the Pentagon had considered them to be all along.

The change in rhetoric was immediately apparent. Just weeks after 9/11, Colombian army officials released a tape of an alleged radio conversation between the FARC military commander, Jorge Briceño, known as Mono Jojoy, and his top lieutenants, in which he was apparently saying that the FARC intended 'to combat [US government personnel] wherever they may be, until we get to their own territory, to make them feel the pain that they have inflicted on other people.'[26] The threat was nonsensical, for it is widely acknowledged that the FARC do not have the capability to achieve a military victory in Colombia, let alone launch attacks in the United States. Although the authenticity of the tape was never proved, the statement had great publicity value. The US hawks wasted no time in denouncing the FARC as Al Qaida-type terrorists. Senator Robert Graham, Chairman of the Senate Select

Committee on Intelligence, said (somewhat incoherently): 'The FARC are doing the same things as global level terrorists, that is, organising in small cells that don't have contact with each other and depend on a central command to organise attacks, in terms of logistics and finance. It is the same style as Bin Laden.'[27] Francis X. Taylor, the US State Department's top counter-terrorism official, declared the FARC to be 'the most dangerous international terrorist group in the hemisphere'.[28]

The ground was prepared for an announcement at the end of October 2001 by US ambassador Anne Patterson that the government was planning to provide counter-terrorism aid to Colombia. In February 2002 Washington announced an additional $98-million package of aid to arm and train Colombia's 18th Brigade (whose job it is to defend the Caño Limón pipeline in Arauca, which is operated and partly owned by the US oil company Occidental Petroleum). In June 2003 General James Hill, commander of SouthCom, went one step further in the rhetorical drive against FARC 'narco-terrorists' by saying that drugs were a 'weapon of mass destruction'.

In the new anti-terrorism frenzy that had seized Washington, it was no longer necessary to pretend that the Pentagon's main aim was to combat narcotics. In April 2004 the Colombian authorities announced Plan Patriota, an ambitious plan that openly set out to defeat the FARC.[29] Without reference to counter-narcotics, General James Hill said that the funding of $100 million over three years would be used to train and equip Colombian troops to do battle with the FARC, particularly in the southern departments of Amazonas and Caquetá (where many FARC troops are reported to have fled after the reverses they suffered in Putumayo). Part of the initial funding would be spent on communications equipment and six new attack planes, to be purchased from US manufacturers. General Hill also speculated that, in future, funds might be directed exclusively to Plan Patriota. The genie was well and truly out of the bottle.

One of the most alarming consequences of the current emphasis on the 'war on terror' has been the tendency to stigmatise all opponents as allies of the insurgents. Human rights activists, environmentalists and those working for non-governmental organisations have all been branded 'terrorists' by high-level members of the Uribe administration. At a conference in Washington in 2002 hosted by the US army, General José Arturo Camelo, head of the Colombian Military Penal Justice division, accused human rights bodies of carrying out a 'judicial war' against the military and of being 'friends of the subversives'.[30] Pedro Juan Moreno, security and intelligence adviser to President Uribe, accused NGOs of acting as front organisations for insurgent groups and said that they were thus legitimate targets for the Colombian military.[31] Fernando Londoño, Uribe's interior minister, said that Colombia was 'the victim of an international conspiracy in which environmentalists and communists participate'.[32] President Uribe himself also claimed that 'when terrorists start feeling weak, they immediately send their spokesmen to talk about human rights', and, although he admitted that some human rights groups were 'respectable', he accused others of being 'political agitators in the service of terrorism, cowards who wrap themselves in the banner of human rights in order to win back for Colombian terrorism the space which the armed forces and the public have taken from it.'[33]

This fiercely combative mentality, which is highly intolerant of criticism, makes it difficult for Colombians to discuss calmly and rationally with the authorities any proposal for an alternative approach to the drug question. Such a discussion is urgently required because, despite the millions of dollars spent on Plan Colombia and the reported reduction in coca cultivation, cocaine trafficking is thriving in Colombia. Numbering perhaps as many as 400, the baby cartels are commercially sophisticated organisations that have a strictly businesslike approach and which have eshewed personality cults.[34] They are service providers of an illegal commodity and are not interested in controlling the whole chain. Because there are so many of them, they are extremely difficult to control.

The Bush administration's emphasis on counter-insurgency does not mean that no serious attempt is being made in the US administration to combat drug trafficking. Members of the Drug Enforcement Agency (DEA), the federal agency in charge of drug law enforcement, are making real efforts to dismantle the new networks. Some members of Congress support them. But the DEA repeatedly clashes with the Defense department, which is focused on the terrorist threat and, in today's climate, is more powerful. Washington has generally gone along with Uribe's misleading claim that 'if Colombia did not have drugs, it would not have terrorists'.[35] It is a myth that suits them both, for it enables them to fuse the military and counter-narcotics aspects of Plan Colombia. It suggests, without quite saying it, that the reverse is true, namely that 'if Colombia did not have terrorists, it would not have drugs'. It is far more acceptable internationally to be deluging the land with poison in pursuit of first a 'war on drugs' and now a 'war on terror' than to admit to be causing this devastation to further the economic and military interests of US corporations and a tiny Colombian elite.

The real objective of Plan Colombia is to defeat the FARC, to drive peasant and indigenous families off land rich in economic resources, to integrate Colombia within the US empire and to groom the country for a key role in US expansionist plans for South America. Plan Colombia can thus be seen, as one writer has put it, as a programme for 'militarised structural adjust-ment', that is, the forced imposition of neoliberal policies.[36] Even before Plan Colombia, the economic element was already in place, for in 1999 Colombia had received a $2.7 billion loan from the IMF and was carrying out the tough, market-oriented economic policies (including the privatisation of state companies) that are invariably the condition for such finance.

Plan Colombia provided the military element to defeat, or at least to weaken, the guerrillas and to clear the way for the take-over of key economic resources by multinational companies.

Colombia's economic resources are in themselves important to the United States, particularly in view of the uncertainty in the Middle East. In late 2001 US ambassador Anne Patterson said that Colombia had 'the potential to export more oil to the United States and, now more than ever, it's important for us to diversify our sources of oil.'[37] Marc Grossman, US Under-Secretary of State for Political Affairs, was even more explicit about the threat that the guerrillas represent to US oil interests when, in a statement to a US Congressional Committee in April 2002, he said that the Colombian insurgents:

> represent a danger to the $4.3 billion in direct US investment in Colombia. They regularly attack US interests, including the railway used by the Drummond Coal mining facility and Occidental Petroleum's stake in the Caño Limón oil pipeline. Terrorist attacks on the Caño Limón pipeline also pose a threat to US energy security. Colombia supplied 3% of US oil imports in 2001, and possesses substantial potential oil and natural gas reserves.[38]

Putumayo is important in this context. Apart from its own considerable oil reserves, it is a hub for regional activities. Four pipelines meet in the remote town of Orito (described in chapter one): two carry oil from nearby fields; another brings oil from the Amazon region of neighbouring Ecuador; and the fourth, called the Transandino, carries oil from the other three pipelines across the Andes to the port of Tumaco. Several international oil companies, including two based in the US, Occidental Petroleum and Argosy Energy, are active in this region. In the 1990s the strong FARC presence disrupted operations. After reaching a high point of 80,000 barrels a day in 1980, oil production fell to just 9,626 barrels a day in 2003. The main reason for the decline was the FARC's success in bombing the pipeline. The number of attacks has fluctuated, reflecting the course of the war, from 48 in 1999 to 110 in 2000, and then, after falling to 43 in 2002, to the record 144 in 2003. Over half of the 2003 attacks occurred in November, when the FARC launched an offensive to demonstrate its continued vitality, despite the onslaught it had suffered from the combined army–paramilitary operations.

The bomb attacks were like waving a red rag to a bull. President Uribe, who until then had concentrated his attention on providing security for the oil multinationals in Arauca, decided it was time to sort out Putumayo. He sacked the local army commander, replacing him with Lieutenant Colonel Cruz, one of the army's crack officers from a counter-insurgency unit. Cruz, who was equipped with advanced weapons and night vision equipment, talked to the press about his mission: 'Security is the most important thing to me. Oil companies need to work without worrying and international investors need to feel calm.'[39] To secure this goal, the Colombian army was prepared to be brutal. General James Hill said that Plan Patriota had begun 'with an attack on rural areas where local peasant farmers support the FARC.'[40] Newspaper reports spoke of 'dozens of raids' and scores of people 'detained on suspicion of giving food and support' to the rebels. Although reliable information was scarce, the army appeared to be applying a scorched earth policy like the one used in Guatemala.

Along with providing greater security for oil companies on the ground, President Uribe also announced in June 2003 far-reaching structural reforms for the oil sector. Whereas in the past oil companies could drill for oil only in joint ventures with the state oil company Ecopetrol, they are now able to own the whole of a venture and to dispose of the oil they produce as they see fit. Even though it had made a healthy profit of $558 million in 2002, Ecopetrol was dismantled. Three smaller companies took over some its tasks, while other functions were discontinued. One of these new companies is running

Ecopetrol's production units for the moment, but it will not be allowed to expand its activities. Although it was not spelt out, it is clear that the government is planning the outright privatisation of the oil industry. The new legislation, with its far more generous conditions for foreign companies, is attracting new investment. In November 2004 Harken Energy, a Texas-based company, announced a new oil exploration contract in Colombia.[41] The company is closely linked to President George W. Bush, who served on its board of directors from 1986 to 1990.

Although Uribe has had considerable success in imposing neoliberalism on the country, it is by no means certain that the military strategy will be successful. During the first years of the Uribe government the FARC appeared to suffer a series of military reversals, being driven back into remote areas. Some members of the government even started speaking confidently of the possibility of defeating the FARC outright, not merely driving them into peace negotiations from a weakened position, as has had been Uribe's original goal. At the time Alfredo Rangel, a leading Colombian military analyst, repeatedly warned the government against being 'triumphalist': 'The FARC have survived for over 40 years,' he said. 'It's important not to lose sight of the kind of war they are waging. They are not seeking to confront the armed forces but to exhaust them. They are biding their time until the military offensive loses steam. They have done this repeatedly in the past.'[42] Indeed, while the government was trumpeting its successes, there were also reports that the FARC were recruiting well in some areas of the country. This would scarcely be surprising, given the large number of families displaced by the violence and the high level of unemployment in the country. In February 2005 came the first confirmation that Rangel was right in his analysis: the FARC launched a series of devastating attacks on the military, killing some 50 soldiers in various regions of the country. In July 2005 the FARC imposed another 'armed blockade' along the main roads in Putumayo, forcing the government to airlift food to the isolated towns. It was a dramatic demonstration of the FARC's continued strength in the department, after almost five years of Plan Colombia.

Notes

1 United States Senate Committee on Armed Services, *Advance Questions for Lieutenant General Peter Pace*, 2000, http://armed-services.senate.gov/statemnt/2000/000906pp.pdf

2 Robert W. Adams, *Memorandum to Mr. Mann, Subject: Helicopters for Colombia*, May 14, 1964; quoted in Doug Stokes, *America's Other War – Terrorizing Colombia*, Zed Books, London, 2005, p. 129.

3 United States Senate Committee on Armed Services, op. cit.

4 International Crisis Group, *War and Drugs in Colombia*, Latin America Report no. 11, January 27, 2005, p. 15.

5 Maria Clemencia Ramírez Lemus, Kimberly Stanton and John Walsh, 'Colombia: A Vicious Circle of Drugs and War', in Coletta A. Youngers and Eileen Rosin, *Drugs and Democracy in Latin America – The Impact of US Policy*, Lynne Rienner Publishers, Boulder, 2005, p. 107.

6 John Waghelstein, Military Review, February 1987, quoted in Doug Stokes, op. cit., p. 131.

7 *El Tiempo*, Bogotá, 15 June 2003.

8 Latin America Weekly Report, London, February 1, 2005.

9 Statement made before the Senate Caucus on International Narcotics Control, September 21, 1999.

10 Gary Leech, 'Plan Colombia: A Closer Look', *Colombia Journal*, New York, July 2000.

11 Ibid.

12 John Lindsay-Poland, 'US Military Bases in Latin America and the Caribbean', *Foreign Policy in Focus*, vol. 3, no. 3, August 2004.

13 Quoted in TNI Briefing Series, 'Forward Operation Locations in Latin America: Transcending Drug Control', 2003, Amsterdam, available on http://www.tni.org/reports/drugs/debate8.pdf

14 John Lindsay-Poland, op. cit.

15 TNI Briefing Series, op. cit., p. 3.

16 See Human Rights Watch, *The 'Sixth Division' – Military–paramilitary Ties and US Policy to Colombia*, September 2001, p. 18.

17 International Crisis Group, op. cit., p. 19.

18 Gary Leech, 'The Paramilitary Spearhead of Plan Colombia', *Colombia Journal*, New York, November 20, 2000.

19   Karl Penhaul, 'Outlaw role seen in Colombia effort', *Boston Globe*, March 28, 2001.

20   Human Rights Watch, op. cit., p. 37.

21   Quoted in Gary Leech, 'The War on Terror in Colombia', *Colombia Journal*, New York, 2004, p. 25.

22   Ibid. p. 35.

23   Quoted in Center for International Policy, *Plan Colombia and Beyond*, December 17, 2004. http://ciponline.org/colombia/blog/

24   United States, General Accounting Office, 'Financial and Management Challenges Continue to Complicate Efforts to Reduce Illicit Drug Activities in Colombia: Statement of Jess T. Ford, Director, International Affairs and Trade', *GAO-03-820T*, Washington, June 3, 2003.

25   Mercopress – the South Atlantic's news agency, August 5, 2005.

26   Quoted in Gary Leech, 'The War on Terror in Colombia', p. 27.

27   Ibid. p. 27.

28   Ibid. p. 27.

29   *El Tiempo*, April 22, 2004.

30   Quoted in Doug Stokes, op. cit., p. 127.

31   *El Espectador*, November 24, 2002; quoted in Doug Stokes, op. cit., p. 127.

32   *EcoNoticias*, July 16, 2002, quoted in Doug Stokes, op. cit., p. 128.

33   Quoted in *Counterpunch*, Petrolia, Calif., September 20, 2003.

34   International Crisis Group, op. cit., p. 21.

35   From a speech to the OAS Permanent Council in Washington, 25 March 2004.

36   Andy Higginbottom, 'Globalisation and Human Rights in Colombia: Crimes of the Powerful, Corporate Complicity and the Paramilitary State', unpublished Ph.D thesis, Middlesex University, 2005. p. 13.

37   Quoted by Gary Leech, 'Plan Petroleum in Putumayo', *Colombia Journal*, May 10, 2004.

38   Marc Grossman, *Testimony of Ambassador Marc Grossman before the House Appropriations Committee's Subcommittee on Foreign Operations*, 10 April 2002; quoted in Doug Stokes, op. cit, p. 124.

39   Ibid.

40   James J. Brittain, 'The Objective Reality of Plan Patriota', *Colombia Journal*, January 24, 2005.

41   Gary Leech, 'Plan Colombia Benefits US Oil Companies', *Colombia Journal*, November 12, 2004.

42   James J. Brittain, op. cit.

4
Administering
the Poison

A great deal of secrecy surrounds the exact chemical formula of the poison that is being poured on to the land to kill the coca bushes. What is known for certain is that the basis for the spray is a well-known weed-killer, Roundup, which is being used with additives in the fumigations. Roundup was developed from the chemical glyphosate by the US pesticide manu-facturer, Monsanto. Roundup is the best-selling farming chemical ever, outselling other agricultural products by five to one.[1] It was for many years marketed as a 'wonder product', said to be both effective in controlling weeds and relatively harmless to the environment and to human health. In its advertising literature, Monsanto described it as 'a non-selective herbicide widely used because of its efficacy and environmental profile. It is the herbicide of choice for conservation tillage.'

Roundup is widely used in many countries and has over the years been a very profitable product for Monsanto, bringing in $2.8 billion in sales in the fiscal year ending August 31, 2000. That year Roundup accounted for about half of Monsanto's income, and even competitors marvelled at its popularity.[2] However, in the autumn of 2000 the US patent expired. As Roundup faced competition from other glyphosate-based herbicides produced by rival companies, Monsanto's sales of the product fell from $2.5 billion in fiscal 2001 to $1.8 billion in fiscal 2003.[3]

The setback proved temporary, with sales bouncing back by 14% in 2004, as Monsanto profited from the expansion of genetically modified crops, particularly Roundup Ready, a strain of soya specially engineered by Monsanto to be resistant to Roundup herbicide. Indeed, some commentators believe that the main reason why Monsanto developed genetically modified soya in the first place was not because it had a higher yield than conventional soya (as Monsanto claimed) but to boost its pesticide sales.[4] Monsanto has lobbied hard to get GM crops authorised in the main farming nations throughout the world and has consistently sought to take over the seed production sector in all the key countries so that soon farmers will have no option but to purchase its GM seeds. Now that Brazil – which had held out against authorising GM crops – has finally succumbed, Monsanto has got its way in every major exporter of agricultural produce.

Monitoring the damage

Monsanto claims that Roundup, used as it is recommended to be used, is safe, but Colombians have repeatedly protested about the harm that the spraying is doing to their health and to the environment. It has been extremely difficult to find out why this should be happening. The Colombian government has refused to disclose the exact formulation of the chemicals that are being sprayed on the land and has so far failed to carry out a proper enquiry into the impact of the spraying. Despite all the difficulties, a few courageous and determined individuals in local governments and in non-governmental organisations have carried out their own surveys, and it is to these that we now turn.

In late 2000 the public health services in the department of Putumayo were inundated with complaints about the impact of the spraying that had commenced in the valleys of the Guamuez, San Miguel and Orito rivers on 18 December. No fewer than 5,929 people from 282 villages (nearly half of the total number of villages in the area) reported ill effects, with

4,883 (81.5%) of complainants saying that they were suffering from medical conditions that they had never experienced before. The main problems they complained of were: respiratory (29%), gastro-intestinal (26%) and dermatological (16%). The hospital in the town of La Hormiga, in the centre of the spraying area, registered a particularly high number of complaints. In response, the public health department in the region decided to carry out an extensive survey into the impact of the spraying.[5] Its researchers painted a dire picture: 12,836 hectares of farmland had been sprayed, with widespread damage to pasture, coca bushes, maize, yucca and fruit trees; and families reported the death of 373,944 animals, mainly fish (301,297), but also pigs, horses, rabbits and doves.

Although the government has often claimed that the spray planes target only large, commercial plantations of coca, this was not the case in this part of Putumayo. The *Comité Andino de Servicios* (Andean Services Committee) had earlier investigated the socio-economic condition of the inhabitants living in the region around La Hormiga. Their interviewees – 1,356 people in 30 villages – had the typical profile of the rural poor: almost two-thirds had not completed primary education, most were of mixed race, two-thirds cooked on wood stoves, most (82%) kept animals in their houses, a third had no form of sanitation whatsoever, and so on. It seems that most coca growers in the whole of Putumayo are similarly poor: another survey carried out in 1996 showed that of the 11,884 hectares of coca cultivation around Puerto Asís, the largest town in Putumayo, less than a quarter were in the hands of large farmers, with an average holding of 18 hectares; about 40% of the families were occupying small plots, with an average size of 2.3 hectares.[6] Coca growers are not getting rich at the expense of consumers of cocaine worldwide, as some advocates of spraying would have us believe.

Because of the difficulties faced by researchers in Colombia, no studies have been able to demonstrate conclusively that the harm suffered by the peasant families is caused by the spraying. Much better information on this topic is to be found in Ecuador, Colombia's southern neighbour. The Ecuadorean province of Sucumbíos lies just south of the Colombian department of Putumayo. The two territories have much in common: most of the inhabitants are poor peasant families; they speak Spanish and have a similar culture; and for many kilometres they share the San Miguel river, which forms the border between the two countries. Until recently, however, one of the things that distinguished Ecuador from its much larger northern neighbour was the unwillingness of its inhabitants to plant coca bushes. Even so, the Ecuadoreans in Sucumbíos have been affected by the spraying, because the wind has blown the herbicide across the river. Because the Ecuadorean authorities do not share the Colombian government's desire to avoid an aerial spraying scandal, scientists have been much freer to carry out research into the impact of the chemicals on people and the environment.

Ecuadoreans have had considerable experience of environmental disasters. Texaco (now part of the TexacoChevron Corporation), the US oil company that for many years exploited the oilfields around Lago Agrio, left the region in a shockingly polluted state. In 2003 some 30,000 Ecuadorean peasants and Indians decided to file for damages in US courts, claiming that between 1964 and 1992 the company had dumped 18 million gallons of toxic waste into hundreds of open pits, estuaries and rivers, and had spilt 16.8 million gallons of crude oil, half as much again as seeped out of the tanker Exxon Valdez in Alaska in 1989. The toxic waste – a chemical stew of heavy metals – had poisoned the land, caused illness, and severely affected the life of indigenous communities. Dave Russell, an Atlanta-based toxics specialist, told the *Wall Street Journal*: 'To put this in perspective, you're looking at something, size-wise, larger than the Chernobyl disaster. The damage is to the entire ecosystem.'[7] At the time of writing, the court case has not ended, but the claimants are hoping that ChevronTexaco will have to pay billions of dollars in compensation. This experience means that Ecuadorean environmental organizations, such as Acción Ecológica, are thoroughly familiar with the techniques of collecting data about pollution. It is thanks to their efforts, coordinated by Dr Adolfo Maldonado, the Spanish doctor that one of the authors (Hugh O'Shaughnessy) met in the small Ecuadorean town of General Farfán, that there is a comprehensive record of the impact of the spraying in northern Ecuador, and to some extent in Putumayo itself.

The first complaints to be registered in Ecuador about the impact of the spraying came from the tiny village of Mataje in the province of Sucumbíos. In October 2000, 44 out of the 154 inhabitants of the hamlet went to the local health centre to complain about red eyes, skin irritation, vomiting and diarrhoea. In December dozens of people went to the Marco Vinicio Iza hospital in Lago Agrio to get treatment for skin infections and respiratory difficulties, as the doctor in charge has confirmed. Although Gwen Claire, the US ambassador in Quito, asserted emphatically that the health problems could not be caused by the spraying and repeated the old claim that glyphosate has 'the same effect as ordinary salt or aspirin and is less harmful than nicotine and Vitamin A',[8] her statement was soon challenged by Dr Marco Álvarez, the Ecuadorean health minister. He said that there was considerable scientific evidence that glyphosate could attack mucous tissues, affect the blood and facilitate the development of bowel cancer.[9]

Acción Ecológica began to carry out its own investigations, with the help of Dr Maldonado. The doctor decided to examine and interview 47 women living on both sides of the border. He chose women because they, unlike their husbands, did not habitually handle the agricultural chemicals used in the fields and it was thus easier to rule out other sources of contamination. Twenty-two of the women (10 in Ecuador and

12 in Colombia) reported spraying on their land. The women living in Colombia had been affected directly. The women in Ecuador, all of whom lived within three kilometres of the border, had noted chemicals drifting over their land. The remaining 25 women, all Ecuadoreans, who acted as a control group, lived about 80 kilometres from the border and had not suffered from the spraying. Maldonado took blood samples from all the women and gave them to Dr César Paz y Miño, at the Pontifical Catholic University of Ecuador (PUCE) in Quito. This specialist decided to carry out so-called 'comet tests' to see if the women's chromosomes had been damaged.

In today's world, it is normal for about 4% of a person's cells to register some form of damage. The 25 Ecuadorean women in the control group were found to have cell damage close to this level (6.93%). But the 22 women, both Colombian and Ecuadorean, who had been affected by the sprayings were found to have suffered much greater genetic damage: more than one third (36.45%) of their cells were damaged. The woman with the most damaged cells, a 23-year-old Colombian, had 85.3% of her cells damaged, 21 times the normal level.[10]

Dr Maldonado's findings were incorporated into a larger report drawn up by a group of Ecuadorean organisations. Bringing together various studies, it concluded:

> After the fumigations, illnesses previously unknown to the population have arisen and it has been possible to note systemic damage in the people, such as respiratory, skin and digestive infections, and nervous complaints. The local inhabitants say that the intensity of some of these illnesses is uncommon for the region. … The results found in the blood analyses indicate that the population living near the frontier are exposed, as the result of the level of chromosome damage, to a greater risk of developing cancer, mutations and congenital malformations. The fumigations may be the cause of the chromosome aberrations.[11]

While these studies are cause for great concern, they are

inconclusive, as the researchers themselves would be the first to admit. What is urgently required is a comprehensive, public and impartial study of the impact of the spraying on the health of the local populations and the environment. Despite frequent requests from social movements, the Colombian authorities refused to carry out such an investigation. Finally, in April 2005, an international study was published that was intended to put an end to the wrangling between critics and supporters of fumigation.[12] Based on scientific evidence, it was supposed to establish once and for all whether or not spraying harmed human health and the environment. It had been quite a struggle to get the authorities to agree to an investigation. It was first proposed in 2001 by Clare Short when she was British minister for overseas development. Aware of both the number of complaints that had been lodged about the spraying in southern Colombia, particularly in the department of Putumayo, and the widespread scepticism that had greeted the various official reassurances that no real harm was being done, she committed her government to providing £100,000 towards the costs of an impartial study. She originally suggested that the investigation should be carried out by the United Nations, but this proposal was immediately rebuffed by the Colombian government. It seems that Klaus Nyholm, the UNDCP (United Nations Drug Control Programme) representative at the time, had antagonized the Colombian authorities by saying that in his view aerial spraying should not be used against small farmers who had little alternative but to cultivate coca and poppies (from which heroin is produced).[13] So in the end the study was commissioned from a team of international researchers under the auspices of the Inter-American Drug Abuse Control Commission (known from its initials in Spanish as CICAD), an agency of the Washington-based Organisation of American States (OAS).

In the past the OAS has tended to endorse US policy uncritically. Readers with long memories will recall that in the

1970s and 1980s the OAS was indulgent towards US-backed military dictatorships while strongly critical of administrations, like Fidel Castro's, which dared to defy Washington. Even so, given the number of fairly prestigious scientists involved in this study, the unequivocal nature of the report's main conclusion came as a surprise: 'The panel concluded that the risks for people and for human health in the use of glyphosate and Cosmo-Flux [the main additive] in the eradication of coca and poppies in Colombia were minimal.'[14] But, far from ending the controversy, this dogmatic statement sparked off a further round of attacks and counter-attacks.

The report's reliability was immediately questioned by Colombian NGOs. The National University of Colombia's Environmental Studies Institute published a detailed and damning analysis of the report.[15] Among other criticisms, it pointed out that the study was not based on an analysis of the impact of the mix of herbicides on actual Colombian families but was based on secondary sources, that is, studies made elsewhere of the impact of glyphosate and Cosmo-Flux. Not surprisingly, it expressed particular concern over the fact that half of the data used in the report was taken from Monsanto. Ricardo Vargas, a leading Colombian authority on narcotics, published a briefer and more outspoken critique of the report.[16] After examining the methodology, Vargas concluded that the report had been specifically designed to reach the pre-determined conclusion that the spraying was harmless.

So, far from resolving the controversy, the report has stoked the fires. Perhaps its greatest weaknesses are its lacunae: the researchers did not demand that the Colombian government reveal to them the exact composition of the combination of herbicides that is being applied today (something that still remains a mystery); they did not directly measure farmers' exposure to the substance, so, as they note, uncertainty remains about the chronic health effects, the genetic mutation and the cancer that may be caused by the spraying; they did not investigate any of the 8,000 health-related complaints that Colombians living in the areas being sprayed have made to the *Fiscalía del Pueblo* (Ombudsman's Office); and they paid no attention to the social and political conditions in which the spraying is occurring (even though, as we shall show later, these are central to the issue). For many Colombians it is hard to escape the conclusion that, far from being 'purely scientific' as the researchers claimed, the report had taken a profoundly political stance by endorsing so strongly the harmlessness of the spraying without providing an adequate analysis to back up this position.

The study has international implications. In April 2005, Ecuador's Constitutional Tribunal issued a ruling,[17] in which it recognised that aerial spraying harms the health of people exposed to the herbicide and supported the right of these people to demand action from the government to have their health protected. The Ecuadorean foreign ministry is now calling on the Colombian authorities to stop spraying within ten kilometres of the frontier with Ecuador, and it has made it clear that, if this request is not granted, it will lodge an international complaint.[18] Indeed, it has already taken the first step, with the Ecuadorean government's Ombudsman's Office presenting the case before the Human Rights Commission of the OAS. The Office based its arguments on the scientific tests carried out by the Genetics Laboratory of the PUCE, coordinated by Dr Adolfo Maldonado.

As the Transnational Institute, an independent research body based in Amsterdam, has pointed out: 'The complaint before the OAS could turn into a theoretical confrontation between the CICAD and Catholic University studies, which represent two different interpretations of the same situation. One must be very optimistic to think that the OAS would admit that the Ecuadoreans are right.'[19] The Ecuadorean government has said that, if its claim is rejected by the OAS, it could lodge a complaint with other bodies, such as the World

Health Organisation (WHO) or even the International Court of Justice in the Hague.

Some Colombians believe that their government should give in to the pressure and carry out a full investigation. In an open letter in May 2005, Alberto Rueda, the former Colombian government adviser and expert on drug policy, pressed the government to carry out a proper study. He recognised that such a study would be difficult to accomplish: it would require extensive institutional capacity (partly because much of the spraying takes place in remote areas controlled by the guerrilla forces) and it would take time, because of the need to identify the risk factors and to monitor the longer-term impact of the chemical substances.[20] But until such a study is carried out, the claims and counter-claims will continue to rage, with no way of resolving the dispute.

Colombia's toxic mix

Why is the spraying doing so much damage in Colombia, if the main ingredient used is Roundup, which the manufacturer repeatedly says is harmless?

Roundup (like all other pesticides and herbicides) has two kinds of ingredients – active and inert. The active ingredients are those designed to kill the targeted pest or plant; the inert ingredients are added to the product either to make the active ingredients easier to apply or to increase their herbicidal effect. As we have noted, the active ingredient in Roundup is glyphosate, long assumed to be relatively harmless. When the US Environmental Protection Agency (EPA) approved glyphosate for general use, it repeated Monsanto's claim that Roundup was 'less toxic than common salt, aspirin, caffeine, nicotine and even Vitamin A', a statement that can be found in a fact sheet on the aerial eradication programme published on the Colombian embassy's website.[21] (However, it is interesting to note that in 1996 the New York State Attorney General won an injunction against Monsanto for falsely claiming that Roundup was 'as safe as table salt'.)[22]

There are several reasons why Roundup is having such serious effects in Colombia. First of all, it is not being applied in Colombia under 'present and expected conditions of use'.[23] Monsanto's own label warns against applying the herbicide 'in a way that will contact workers or other persons, either directly or through drift'.[24] The label also calls on farmers to remove livestock prior to spraying, to wait for two to eight weeks before harvesting crops, and to avoid herbicide contact with foliage, green stems, desirable trees and plants 'because severe injury or destruction may result'.[25] As a report published by the US Institute for Science and Interdisciplinary Studies (ISIS) points out, 'these conditions are not met in Colombia, where airplanes apply herbicides over acres at a time with no prior warning to landowners. In the US, such failure to follow the label instructions would be a violation of federal law.'[26]

There are, moreover, other factors that exacerbate the damage. Until 2004 the herbicide used in Colombia was Roundup Ultra, composed of 41% glyphosate, 14.5% surfactant and 44.5% water.[27] The surfactant, which helps to spread the glyphosate evenly on the targeted plants and increases its toxicity, was believed to be polyoxyethyleneamine (POEA), although Monsanto did not reveal its exact identity.[28]

Although the US State Department steadfastly refused publicly to admit that this formulation might be harmful to human health, it quietly moved to a more benign formulation after pressure from the Environmental Protection Agency (EPA). According to a report on the US State Department website, now removed, the EPA recommended that '…due to the acute eye irritation caused by the concentrated glyphosate formulated product and the lack of acute toxicity data on the tank mixture, the Agency recommends that DoS [the US Department of State] consider using an alternative glyphosate product (with lower potential for acute toxicity) in future coca and/or poppy aerial eradication programs.'[29] As the report itself made explicit, this recommendation was being made to address the risk that plane operators might accidentally splash the full-strength glyphosate into their eyes or on to their skin as they filled the spray tanks in their planes. It was not directed at the much greater risk experienced by peasant families who might be splashed with – or even completely covered in – the herbicide as the planes sprayed the crops.

According to the US State Department report, at the time the EPA made this recommendation, there were no alternative glyphosate formulations registered for sale and use in Colombia that offered lower potential for acute eye irritation. So, the report continues, the Department of State worked with the programme's glyphosate supplier to find an alternative and, as soon as this was available, began to purchase it for use in the spray programme. It remains, the report says, the formulation used today.

The report does not name the new formulation but gives some clues: like the previous formulation, the new formulation is also registered with the EPA for sale in the US for non-agricultural use and it also contains 41% glyphosate salt and 59% inert ingredients. The difference between the formulations is that the current product has an overall category III toxicological rating ('mildly toxic') on the scale used by the EPA, whereas the previously used glyphosate formulation was rated category I ('highly toxic'). Although no one can be sure, it is likely that one of the weaker versions of Roundup – probably Roundup Pro or Roundup Weathermax – is now being used. By accepting the need for change, the US State Department was tacitly accepting that Roundup Ultra was too aggressive.

In Colombia, however, there is another complicating factor. Although the label for Roundup Ultra warns that 'this is an end-use product. Monsanto does not intend and has not registered it for reformulation',[30] at least one additive – known by the brand name Cosmo-Flux 411F – has been routinely mixed into the spraying solution. Most observers believe that, despite the changes in 2004, this is still the case.

Dr Elsa Nivia, director of the Colombian branch of the Pesticide Action Network, who carries out research from her laboratory in Cali, believes that, irrespective of the exact formulation of Roundup that is being used, there is cause for concern. First, she says, the main tests for Roundup were carried out on rats, and she challenges the widespread assumption that human beings respond in the same way as rats do to this herbicide. She has analysed data from the scientific literature on cases in which humans have died from Roundup ingestion and has calculated that glyphosate appears to be up to 22 times as toxic to humans as to rats.[31] Secondly, she believes that the POEA surfactant is up to five times as toxic as the glyphosate itself.[32] Thirdly, she considers that the dosage and the intensity of aerial spraying carried out in Colombia greatly increase the harm caused. Using information she obtained from officials participating in the eradication programme, she calculates that spray planes deposit what amounts to a 26% concentration of glyphosate, compared to the 1% recommended in the US for weed control in crops. And finally, she believes that, if a fourfold increase in the impact of the herbicide is factored into the calculations because of the addition of Cosmo-Flux, which she says is a reasonable hypothesis, then the overall impact of the chemical mixture could be up to 104 times as great as that of Roundup in normal agricultural practice.[33] In 2001, following the publication by Hugh O'Shaughnessy of an article in the *Observer* on the harmful impact of the spraying,[34] the British chemical company ICI, the manufacturer of one of the ingredients of Cosmo-Flux, stopped supplying the chemical to the Colombians.[35] As reports suggest that Cosmo-Flux is still being added, it must be assumed that another supplier was found.

One of the most worrying aspects of the whole situation is

the secrecy. The US Congress established laws and rules under which the fumigation is supposed to take place in Colombia. The lack of transparency raises serious doubts as to whether these conditions are being met. At the same time, the US authorities are obliged to produce a detailed assessment of the environmental impact of the exact mix that is being applied. Although the US State Department has quietly adapted the formula in response to EPA concerns, it has never published this report.

In line with Dr Elsa Nivia's concerns, evidence is appearing in other parts of the world that even without additives glyphosate may not be as harmless as manufacturers have been claiming. Data from the Department of Pesticide Regulation in California, published in 1998, showed that glyphosate had caused more pesticide-induced illnesses than any other herbicide.[36] Symptoms included swollen eyes, faces and joints, facial numbness, burning and itching skin, blisters, rapid heart rate, raised blood pressure, chest pains, congestion and nausea. A 1999 study found that people exposed to glyphosate were 2.7 times as likely to contact non-Hodgkin's lymphoma as the control group.[37] In 2000 an epidemiological study of the farming populations in Ontario, Canada showed that glyphosate nearly doubled the risk of late spontaneous abortions (miscarriages).[38] And in 2003 a further study suggested that, probably because of the surfactant POEA, Roundup was more toxic than glyphosate alone.[39]

One European government is taking measures to ensure that Roundup does not contaminate its country's drinking water. In May 2003, following publication of data showing the chemical's presence in the groundwater from which Denmark obtains its drinking water without the need of filter beds, Hans Christian Schmidt, the environment minister, announced an inquiry. The background to his decision was reported in the Copenhagen daily newspaper *Politiken*:

Denmark's most popular herbicide, Roundup, is polluting the underground water far more than previously thought. About 800 tonnes of active glyphosate in herbicides are used in agriculture each year.... The chemical glyphosate, which is found in the popular herbicides Roundup and Touchdown, is, against all expectations, leaching down through the soil and polluting the groundwater, so that it contains more than five times the level of glyphosate permitted for drinking water. This has been shown from tests done by the Denmark and Greenland Geological Research Institution (DGGRI) in an as yet unpublished article. It was the Environment Ministry that authorised the use of glyphosate, based on the producer's [Monsanto's] own research.

Farmers spray glyphosate on their fields after the harvest to keep the soil free of twitch weeds and thistles. Earlier studies showed that wells in the Roskilde and Storstroms regions, as well as in the Copenhagen district council area, had been contaminated. Critics say glyphosate causes cancer, while its defenders call it a wonder herbicide. ... 'The results show that glyphosate is polluting our drinking water and unfortunately we have only seen the tip of the iceberg, because glyphosate and many other spray chemicals are at this moment on their way through the soil. Politicians need to look at agriculture in relation to clean drinking water and decide what they are going to do', says Mogens Henze [a professor of environment and resources at the Technical University of Denmark], who says that the farmers cannot be blamed for using something that the authorities have permitted.[40]

In June 2003 the Danish environment minister announced new restrictions for glyphosate, a precedent that may eventually be followed in other European countries. Since 1993 the privatised Welsh Water company has been finding greater traces of glyphosate in the water than those permitted in European Union legislation.[41] In television advertisements for Roundup screened in Britain in 2004, Monsanto was required to warn the viewer that the product 'contains glyphosate'. These are clearly the first signs of official concern. Indeed,

European government officials have privately told the authors that, whatever mix of glyphosate being used, they would never authorise the fumigation of EU territory.

Speaking out

Despite the high levels of violence, corruption and lawlessness, Colombia has an extremely vibrant civic society, and many courageous individuals, working inside the government and outside it, have done what they can to get the authorities to act more responsibly.[42]

In the first place, they have denounced the fact that those in charge of the eradication programme are not respecting even the country's own regulations. After a strongly worded complaint from one of the country's leading human rights organisations, La Corporación Colectivo de Abogados José Alvear Restrepo (CCAJAR), Dr Isabel Cristina Ruiz, the Director General of Public Health, the most senior post in the health ministry, acknowledged in a letter in October 2002 that, according to regulations dating from 1991, the spraying of weed-killers was not permitted from a distance of more than 10 metres on land and 100 metres in the air, in order to protect animals, watercourses, roads and human dwellings. These regulations are being routinely flouted by the fumigations. The main anti-drug statute (law 30 of 1986) also requires the prior approval of health and environmental agencies before spraying can be carried out, but this ruling has never been respected. It was not until January 2002, after much to-ing and fro-ing between the different departments, that an environment management plan was put in place. Even now this plan has not been properly enforced, and under the Uribe government some of its provisions have been weakened.

Secondly, non-governmental organisations have repeatedly called for proper monitoring. Along with other bodies, CCAJAR

has published numerous protests, including a booklet titled
Plan Colombia – No, in which it commented:

> There is plenty of money to purchase glyphosate, to maintain the
> planes used in the spraying, to pay the pilots, to build bases where
> they can live, and to carry out operations to detect the coca crops,
> but there are never any resources for evaluating the damage caused
> by glyphosate to the health of Colombians who have been sprayed.

CCAJAR then observed, with considerable bitterness, that it
was perhaps not surprising that the Colombian authorities were
so ineffective, for the spraying was carried out by US
companies, the substance they were using was manufactured
by a US company, and the pilots were US citizens who reported
to the US embassy.

Some local judges have tried to curb the abuses. In a
remarkable judgment on June 13, 2003, the supreme court of
Cundinamarca, a department in the centre of Colombia,
ordered the spraying of chemicals to be halted. In the summary
of the reasons for its decision, the court referred to the study
carried out by Dr Maldonado. But the Uribe government
appealed to the Council of State, a federal court with greater
powers than the local Cundinamarca court, and won the right
to ignore the ruling. In an interview for this book, Diana
Murcia, a lawyer from the CCAJAR, looked at the arguments
that the government presented, and summarises them as
follows:

- A suspension of spraying will benefit armed outlawed
  groups, as the drug business provides them with their
  resources. They have been behind the protests against the
  spraying.
- There is no effective alternative to spraying.
- It is not the glyphosate, but the chemicals used in the
  cultivation of coca bushes and poppies, that damage people's
  health and the environment.

- Plan Colombia is incorporated into Colombian law. If Colombia were to be unable to carry out its obligations under the Plan, 'it would be subject to international reprisals with incalculable consequences.'

Her reply to each of the four points is robust:

- It is an attack on the very idea of citizenship and democracy to suggest that all complainants have links with armed groups. The fumigation has harmed the political, economic, social and cultural rights of many peasants, Indians and Afro-Colombians. Those who complain about the spraying and its impact on human life cannot automatically be stigmatised as drug-traffickers or members of armed groups.
- Aerial eradication is not the only way of waging war on drugs. Manual eradication has worked in many parts of the country. Bad management and poor planning are the reasons why it has failed in other parts of the country.
- While it is true that the growing and processing of drugs have a high environmental cost, it cannot be assumed it is this that has caused the health problems faced by many growers. It is beyond doubt that the mixture of glyphosate, POEA and Cosmo-Flux which is being sprayed on the bushes, can do great harm. The government's position – that those who have been affected need to prove that the damage was caused by the spraying – is unacceptable. It is the duty of the Colombian state to prove that the spraying does no damage. As no environmental risk assessment has been carried out, the principle of precaution has to prevail. The mere indication of environmental damage is enough to justify calls for the government to take remedial action.
- It is unacceptable for the government to allege that it will be subject to reprisals if it halts the spraying. The government must not allow itself to be blackmailed, especially since the

treaties and agreements on which Plan Colombia is based have never been submitted to any constitutional scrutiny.

The controversy over the parks

One of the fiercest debates concerns national parks: should they be excluded from the spraying? The role of these parks, which cover 10 million hectares, is to provide permanent protection to Colombia's biodiversity, considered to be among the richest in the world. On June 27, 2003 in Bogotá, the *Consejo Nacional de Estupefacientes* (the National Narcotics Council) decided that spraying would be permitted. Just a few days later Marta Lucía Hernández, director of the Tayrona National Park on the Caribbean coast, was murdered by paramilitaries. It seemed that the whole park system was under siege.

The protests that followed were deafening. A former environment minister, Juan Mayr, described the proposal to spray national parks as 'an assassination attempt on Colombia's collective heritage'. Carlos Castaño Uribe, who had headed the *Unidad Nacional de Parques Naturales* (the National Department for Nature Reserves) for 15 years, commented: 'The country has made an enormous effort to safeguard these protected areas, because they are the gene bank of the nation. The planet's greatest store of biodiversity cannot be treated in this way.'[43] Daniel Samper Pizano, a noted Colombian writer, pointed out that the protected parks covered no less than 9% of Colombia and that the decision to protect such a large share of national territory had been taken because of the country's rich biodiversity: Colombia boasted 1,754 species of bird, more than any other country, and it had the world's second largest stock of plants and amphibians and the third largest stock of reptiles.[44] He argued that the Uribe government had weakened environmental protection in response to foreign pressure. It had replaced a proper, functioning ministry with a hodgepodge called the Ministry of the Environment, Housing and Territorial Development – a monster, he argued, that could be compared in one's imagination to a Ministry for the Cultivation of Apples, the Teaching of Ballet and Car Repairs. The main reason why Sandra Suárez had been appointed environment minister, he said, was that she had once been director of Plan Colombia, the star achievement of which had been to spray poisons on woods and jungles. 'Where are we going in this mad struggle against poppies and coca bushes?' he asked.

Even former government officials joined the chorus of protests. Ernesto Guhl Nannetti, vice-minister of the environment in the Pastrana government, said that for him the worst thing was to realise that all the environmental damage had been in vain, for drug-trafficking was flourishing as never before. 'The principal winners have been the manufacturers of the chemical agents used for the spraying and the contractors who have carried out the spraying,' he commented bitterly.

> How many more hectares will have to be sprayed? How many more peasants will have to be ruined? How many woods will have to disappear and how many rivers will have to be polluted before the results of the spraying are reviewed publicly and objectively and the struggle against drugs is reorganised so that tackling consumption is allocated a much bigger role? Instead of spraying the parks, wouldn't it be much better to use the money to look after the parks and to strengthen their administration and security?[45]

This outcry had an impact: in March 2004 the Colombian environment minister said that the government would resort to fumigation in national parks only if manual eradication failed. Although the statement fell far short of the watertight ban that the environmentalists wanted, it represented a real advance.

But not for long. In June 2004 a plane belonging to the US contractors DynCorp began spraying an area of the Sierra Nevada de Santa Marta belonging to the Kogui indigenous people. UNESCO had declared this northern park a biosphere reserve in 1986, and the Kogui, with the help of a French NGO, had bought 2,000 hectares of it in 1997, and had then worked to recover the land's biodiversity. In May 2004, just a fortnight before the spraying, the Colombian government recognised their land as a nature reserve. The final irony is that this land contained no coca whatsoever. In May 2005 the Colombian government announced publicly that it planned to fumigate the nature reserves of Sierra Nevada de Santa Marta, La Macarena in the centre-east and Catatumbo in the north-west.

Few environmentalists would deny that there is a problem. Figures from the CIA showed that the area planted with coca in just six of the country's nature reserves increased by 6,550 hectares in 2004. To some extent, this is the result of Plan Colombia itself, which is leading peasant families to plant coca in more remote areas. But most environmentalists propose another solution: manual eradication. They say that this has already proved effective in some parks, and point out that spraying would violate the international treaties on biodiversity that Colombia has signed and the Colombian Constitution, which requires the authorities to reach prior agreement with the communities involved.

After the chemicals, the fungus

As if the glyphosate mix were not doing enough damage, there are now strong indications that Colombia is currently rethinking its earlier decision not to use biological weapons to eradicate coca and opium poppy crops. *Fusarium oxysporum* is a plant pathogen that causes withering, rot and death to a variety of plants. As the active ingredient is a fungus, the plant is technically known as a mycoherbicide (from *myco*, Greek for mushroom). David C. Sands, a plant pathologist at the University of Montana in the US, who has carried out research into *fusarium oxysporum,* calls it 'an Attila the Hun disease', pointing out that there are strains of *fusarium* for virtually every cultivated plant and many wild ones.[46]

The story of US involvement in this story is bizarre. In the early 1980s, the United States Department of Agriculture (USDA) took over a legal coca plantation in Peru, previously owned by Coca Cola, and started to use it to test herbicides. In 1987 a mysterious pathogen infected the control plot, killing most of the coca plants, and the USDA asked Sands for his help. Sands discovered that the plants had been attacked by a naturally occurring pathogen of the *fusarium oxysporum* family. To the US authorities it must have seemed like manna from heaven: a native biological weapon with which to devastate the coca fields. In 1998, the US Congress approved $23 million to fund the development of this fungus to an operational stage. Sands carried out the research in his university.

This was not the first time that a *fusarium* had been developed to combat drugs. In 1999 the US federal government wanted to use another strain of *fusarium* to eradicate marijuana plantations in Florida, but the state department of the Environment Protection Agency refused to give its authorisation. 'It is difficult, if not impossible, to control the dispersal of *fusarium* species,' said the EPA director, explaining his decision. 'The fungus can mutate and damage a wide variety of crops. *Fusarium* species are more active in warm soils and can remain active in the soil for years.' But this did not mean that *fusarium* was automatically ruled out for Colombia. In a letter to President Clinton on August 3, 1999, Senate majority leader Trent Lott and House Speaker Dennis Hastert, both Republicans, called for 'the early deployment of myco-herbicides in FARC- and ELN-controlled zones' in Colombia.

In an edition of the BBC TV programme Panorama transmitted in October 2000, Sands, who had by then set up AgBio/Con, a company that holds patents on ways to disperse mycoherbicides, suggested that large military transport planes should be used to drop massive quantities of *fusarium* spores on coca bushes in Colombia. He said that coca-growing areas should be 'blanketed' with the spores, which would mean that the fungus would get well established, thus making it impossible for the farmer to replant once the planes had left.[47] He favoured such action being taken with or without the permission of the Colombian authorities. At the same time, the US Congress was upping the pressure and saying that Colombia's foreign aid should be made conditional on the use of *fusarium*.[48]

There were at the time several unconfirmed reports that experiments with *fusarium* had already been carried out. According to an article in the *New Herald* (a Miami newspaper) in July 2000, the US army had experimented with the fungus in an area five kilometres north of Lago Agrio in Ecuador, a claim backed by the mayor of Puerto Guzmán.[49] According to Jeffrey St Clair, a prominent US journalist, the US ambassador to Colombia, Anne Patterson, had also testified some time earlier that she believed biological weapons had already been deployed in Colombia. She later retracted her statement, which she said had been made 'under duress' (though she did not specify what kind of duress).[50]

Not surprisingly, the spectre of biological warfare set alarm bells ringing. Several commentators in Colombia and abroad pointed out that the use of *fusarium* spores would almost certainly be a contravention of the UN Biological Weapons Convention. Ecuador and Peru immediately banned the use of mycoherbicides in their territory and Brazil lodged a complaint with the United Nations. After a high-profile public campaign, coordinated by Colombian non-governmental organisations, the United Nations advised against the use of the fungus. In August 2000 President Clinton specifically ruled out US aid to Colombia being made conditional on the use of the fungus. In a resolution in February 2001 the European Parliament declared itself 'convinced that…the [European] Union must take the necessary steps to secure an end to the large-scale use of chemical herbicides and to prevent the introduction of biological agents, such as *Fusarium oxysporum*, given the dangers of their use to human health and the environment alike.'[51] It appeared that good sense had won out, and the controversy died down.

However, the lobby in favour of biological weapons did not accept defeat. At a hearing of the Congressional Committee on Government Reform on December 13, 2002, John Mica, a Republican Congressman for Florida (where environmental and health concerns had led the government to cancel its plans to combat marijuana plantations with *fusarium*), made an impassioned plea. 'We have to restore our…mycoherbicide,' he said. 'Things that have been studied for too long need to be put into action…it would do a lot of damage…it will eradicate some of these crops for substantial periods of time.'[52] In an interview at the US embassy in Bogotá in 2003, Hugh O'Shaughnessy was told by a member of the US team dealing with narcotics that Washington would not seek to use biological agents 'that did not occur naturally'. This statement clearly left the door open to the application of a natural fungal agent, fashioned inside or outside Colombia, such as the *fusarium* that had been developed by Sands.

In fact, it emerged in 2004 that behind-the-scenes investigations into biological weapons had continued. While the UNDCP had distanced itself from the *fusarium* research, it had carried out secret studies, financed by the British government, into the use of another fungus (*Pleospora papaveracea*) to eradicate poppies in Afghanistan.[53] At the same time, the US had pushed ahead quietly with its research into *fusarium*. In March 2004 a Colombian senator leaked to the press a letter written by a US State Department official to the Colombian ambassador in Washington, in which he stated that, in response to a request from President Alvaro Uribe, the US government was 'willing to share' with Colombian officials the latest results of its research into the use of mycoherbicides on coca crops in

Colombia. The Transnational Institute commented: 'The current state of these meetings is not public knowledge, but the fact that they are going on at a time when the Uribe government is waging a full-scale campaign to win an extension for Plan Colombia, which is officially due to end in 2005, is cause for concern.'

Further corroboration that the *fusarium* option was still being actively considered came in June 2005 when Dan Burton, a Republican member of the US Congress, issued a statement in which he said:

> We spend millions of dollars every day on counter-narcotics efforts, including crop eradication and interdiction, especially in our joint efforts in Colombia, Afghanistan and elsewhere, yet the flow of illegal and lethal narcotics continues to be a major problem in our country. The advent of mycoherbicides and other counter-narcotic alternatives offers us the possibility to cut off the source of these drugs literally at their roots.[54]

Supporting his colleague, the Republican Drug Policy Chairman, Mark Souder, added: 'Mycoherbicide research needs to be investigated, and we need to begin testing it in the field.'[55] The Congressmen meant what they said: they managed to introduce into new drug legalisation going through Congress a provision that requires the drawing up of a 'plan of action to conduct controlled scientific testing of naturally existing mycoherbicide in a major drug producing nation' within 90 days of the enactment of the new law. Although it was not spelt out, it seems very likely that the nation to carry out the tests will be Colombia.

Nature fights back

While the controversy over fumigation raged, rumours circulated about the emergence of a new wonder kind of coca, known variously as *supercoca, la millonaria* and *boliviana negra*.[56]

This strain, it was said, grew much taller than conventional coca, produced leaves with a higher cocaine content, and, most important of all, was resistant to Roundup. Speculation was rife that a scientist from one of the biotechnology companies had developed a genetically modified strain of coca. If this were the case, then GM coca would be exactly like Monsanto's GM Roundup Ready soya, in that it would have had a special gene introduced into it to make it resistant to glyphosate. The spraying of Roundup would kill all normal crops but not this coca.

In November 2004 Joshua Davis, a US investigative journalist, travelled to La Hormiga, a town in Putumayo, to track down the *supercoca*. With little difficulty, he found farmers who were cultivating the strain, known in the region as *boliviana negra*. 'Now that we have *boliviana negra*, the herbicide is only affecting legal crops,' a farmer confirmed. 'So the fumigation is encouraging us to plant not our old crops such as yucca, bananas and maize, but the only thing that will survive – *boliviana negra*.' Fabio Paz, the mayor of La Hormiga, confirmed to Davis that farmers were switching in droves to *boliviana negra*. 'You can give away other types of coca now,' he said, because the farmers don't want them. Davis took a sample of *boliviana negra* back to his hotel and carried out a simple laboratory test in his room to see if the coca contained the Roundup Ready gene. Rather to his disappointment, it did not.

This by no means suggests, however, that the coca farmers are lying or misguided in their insistence that *boliviana negra* is resistant to Roundup. As one of the authors (Sue Branford) reported in the *New Scientist*, the repeated application of Roundup herbicide to Roundup Ready soya in Argentina has encouraged the emergence of mutated 'super-weeds' that are resistant to the glyphosate.[57] Such a chance mutation could have occurred in Bolivia or Colombia. Coca growers could have produced seeds from this mutant strain and then distributed them among themselves. If this is the case, as seems likely, the spraying of glyphosate will become a futile exercise and the US government will almost certainly put extra pressure on the Colombian authorities to spray *fusarium* as the only effective way of eradicating coca. *Fusarium* would do more damage even than glyphosate and, worse still, it could become uncontrollable. Because it is a fungus, it could spread rapidly to other crops and to other regions. The idea of *fusarium* spreading widely in the Amazon basin is a truly frightening prospect. The bio-war may be just beginning.

Notes

1   *New York Times*, August 2, 2001.
2   Ibid.
3   *Business Week* online, February 3, 2004.
4   See statement by David Hathaway, quoted in Jeff Conant, *Agent Green over the Amazon*, Green Planet, 2000.
    http://66.102.9.104/search?q=cache:boY2-hg22E8J:www.totse.com/en/politics/green_planet/ 162764.html+David+Hathaway+Roundup+reason+introduction&hl=en&lr=lang_en
5   Departamento administrativo de salud, *Impacto de las fumigaciones aereas con glifosato en el Putumayo*, Subdirección de Salud Pública, Putumayo, Colombia, 2002.
6   Eduardo Alomía, *Estudio de impacto socioambiental generado por el cultivo y proceso de la hoja de coca Erythoxilon coca Lam, en los municipios de Puerto Asís y el Vallle de Guamués, Departamento de Putumayo*, Universidad Inca, Bogotá, 1997.
7   *Wall Street Journal*, 20 October, 2003.
8   Reported in the Quito daily *Expreso*, July 19, 2000.
9   Reported in the Quito daily *Hoy*, September 19, 2000.
10 'Daños Genéticos en la Frontera de Ecuador por las Fumigaciones del Plan Colombia', prepared by Dr Adolfo Maldonado for Dr Claudio Mueckay, Defensoría del Pueblo de Ecuador, investigation file 9067-DAP-2002, November 2003.
11 Amicus Curiae, *Impactos en Ecuador de las fumigaciones a cultivo ilícitos en Colombia*, published by ten Ecuadorean NGOs, including Acción Ecológica, Quito, December 2003.
12 www.cicad.oas.org/es/glisfosatoInformeFinal.pdf
13 Transnational Institute, Drug Policy Briefing, no. 14, June 2005.

14 Inter-American Drug Abuse Control Commission (CICAD), a division of the Organization of American States (OAS), 'Environmental and Human Health Assessment of the Aerial Spray Program for Coca and Poppy Control in Colombia', March 31, 2005, p. 105. www.cicad.oas.org/es/glisfosatoInformeFinal.pdf

15 http://www.idea.unal.edu.co/public/docs/Observ_IDEA_a_doc_CICAD.pdf

16 Ricardo Vargas, 'A few Comments about the OAS–CICAD study of the impact of Glyphosate used in the Eradication of Illicit Crops in Colombia', Transnational Institute, Amsterdam, May 2005. http://www.tni.org/archives/vargas/cidad.htm

17 http://www.llacta.org/organiz/coma/2005/como115.htm

18 See Transnational Institute, Drug Policy Briefing, no. 15, September 2005.

19 Ibid. p. 3.

20 Quoted in Transnational Institute, Drug Policy Briefing, no. 14, June 2005.

21 Quoted on the website of the US embassy in Bogotá, Narcotics Affairs Section, http://usembassy.state.gov/bogota/wwwhglyp.html

22 Quoted in a fact sheet published on the Internet by the Center for Community Action and Environmental Justice (CCAEJ) in California.

23 See G.M. Williams, R. Kroes and J.C. Munro, 'Safety evaluation and risk assessment of the herbicide Roundup and its active ingredient, glyphosate, for humans', *Regulatory Toxicology and Pharmacology*, 31 (2, Pt. 1), 2000, pp. 117–65.

24 Jim Oldhan and Rachel Massey, *Aerial Spraying Review – Health and Environmental Effects of Herbicide Spray Campaigns in Colombia*, Institute for Science and Interdisciplinary Studies (ISIS), March 18, 2002.

25 Ibid.

26 US Institute for Science and Interdisciplinary Studies (ISIS), Health/Environment Factsheet, 'Aerial Spraying in Colombia: Health and Environmental Effects', March 19, 2002. http://isis.hampshire.edu/amazon/colombia/index.php?file=factsheet&title=Health/Environment%20Factsheet

27 Material Safety Data Sheet for Roundup Ultra, available at http://www.cdms.net/idat/mp178020.pdf

28 Oldhan and Massey, op. cit.

29 US State Department, Updated Report on Chemicals Used in the Colombian Aerial Eradication Program http://www.state.gov/g/inl/rls/rpt/aeicc/26581.htm

30 Roundup Ultra sample label, 1999.

31 *Pesticides News*, no. 53, September 2001.

32 Elsa Nivia, 'Aerial spraying of illicit crops is dangerous – some approximations', paper presented in Spanish to the conference Wars in Colombia: Drugs, Guns and Oil, University of California, Davis, May 17–19, 2001.

33 Ibid.

34 Hugh O'Shaughnessy, *Observer*, June 17, 2001.

35 Antony Barnett and Solomon Hughes, 'ICI pulls out of cocaine war', *Observer*, July 1, 2001.

36 Quoted in Chemical Watch fact sheet published on the internet by Beyond Pesticides, Washington, US.

37 Lennart Hardell and Mikael Eriksson, *A Case-Control Study of Non-Hodgkin's Lymphoma and Exposure to Pesticides*, American Cancer Society, Atlanta, 1999.

38 D.A. Savitz *et al.*, 'Male pesticide exposure and pregnancy outcome', *American Journal of Epidemiology*, no. 146, 2000, pp. 1025–36.

39 Quoted in chapter 7 of *The Case for a GM-Free Sustainable World*, ISIS and TWN, London and Penang, 2003.

40 *Politiken*, May 10, 2003.

41 On March 3, 2004 the company confirmed to the author that on June 8, 1995, in a final treated water source, 0.53 ug/l of glyphosate was recorded, more than five times the permitted maximum of 0.1 ug/l. The groundwater source was in the Black Mountains, just outside Abergavenny, Wales. Monsanto visited the site and agreed with Welsh Water's finding.

42 See Maria Clemencia Ramírez Lemus, Kimberly Stanton and John Walsh, 'Colombia: A Vicious Circle of Drugs and War', in Coletta A. Youngers and Eileen Rosin, *Drugs and Democracy in Latin America*, Lynne Rienner Publishers, Boulder and London, 2005, p. 120.

43 *El Tiempo*, Bogotá, January 7, 2004.

44 *El Tiempo*, March 11, 2004.

45 *El Tiempo*, March 9, 2004.

46 Quoted in Jeff Conant, op. cit.

47 Quoted in Martin Jelsma, *Vicious Circle: The Chemical and Biological War on Drugs*, Transnational Institute, Amsterdam, 2001.

48 Transnational Institute, 'Drugs and Conflict in Colombia', http://www.tni.org/drugs/index.htm

49 *New Herald*, Miami, July 21, 2000.

50 *Counterpunch*, Petrolia, Calif., December 31, 2002.

51 European Parliament Resolution on Plan Colombia and Support for the Peace Process in Colombia, February 1, 2001.

52 Quoted in a news release published by The Sunshine Project, a US pressure group, on December 17, 2003.

53 Transnational Institute, 'The Re-emergence of the Biological War on Drugs', Drug Policy Briefing, no. 7, May 2004.

54 Media Advisory Office of Congressman Dan Burton, 'Chairmen Bouton and Souder Praise House Committee Passage of Illegal Drug Crop Reduction Legislation', Washington, June 16, 2005.

55 Ibid.

56 Joshua Davis, 'Colombia: the mystery of the coca plant that wouldn't die', *Wired*, November 1, 2004.

57 Sue Branford, 'Argentina's bitter harvest', *New Scientist*, April 12, 2004.

5
Privatising War

One controversial aspect of the US government's military strategy in Colombia has been the use of private civilian contractors to carry out the aerial spraying of the pesticides and to gather intelligence in conflict zones. According to the US State Department, there are 17 private contractors operating with US government funding in Colombia. Although the US Congress originally ruled that these companies could not employ jointly more than 400 US citizens, it ceded to a request from the Bush administration in October 2004 to raise the cap to 600.

This figure gives a misleading impression of the strength of the private contractors: there is no ceiling on the number of Colombians (or people of other nationalities) who can work for these companies and, although it is extremely difficult to obtain accurate information, the *New York Times* believes that they employ 'hundreds'.[1] According to Ken Silverstein, who has written a book on these private contractors,[2] the companies, led by DynCorp, the large Virginia-based all-purpose contractor, moved into the Andes in the early 1990s, initially working in Peru. They were given US State Department contracts to provide services in the 'war against drugs' but, right from these early days, the distinction between counter-narcotics and counter-insurgency was blurred. In 1992 one of DynCorp's helicopters nose-dived into the jungle in Peru, killing the three men aboard, all of whom were said to be DynCorp employees. According to the US State Department, the crash was caused by 'crew fatigue'. One of the men killed was Robert Hitchman, a covert agent who had worked for the CIA in Laos and Libya. As Ken Silverstein said at the time, 'Hitchman was not in Peru to repair helicopters'.[3] Silverstein spoke to Hitchman's son, who told him that the helicopter had, in fact, been shot down by Shining Path guerrillas, and the US State Department had asked him to keep quiet about the true cause of his father's death.[4]

The operation in Peru was soon eclipsed by the much bigger role that the contractors began to play in Colombia. Even before the announcement of Plan Colombia, some US contractors were providing security for US companies in Colombia. For instance, in 1997 the US security company Airscan was given the job providing security for Occidental Petroleum's oil facilities in Caño Limón in the department of Arauca. In one of the most publicised atrocities of the war, a Colombian air force helicopter dropped a bomb on the hamlet of Santo Domingo in Arauca in December 1998, apparently believing that they were attacking a FARC column. The bomb killed 17 people, including six children. No member of the FARC was killed or injured. It emerged during an investigation that the operation had been planned at Occidental's head-quarters, although none of Airscan's employees participated in the attack.

It was only with the announcement of Plan Colombia, however, that US contractors began to play a big role. Although the contractors are supposed only to be flying spray planes, several reliable journalists have reported on their involvement in other tasks, such as bugging phones and gathering and assessing intelligence, which suggests that they have also been involved in counter-insurgency.[5] It is difficult to obtain accurate information, but at least six other labour contractors (besides DynCorp) are believed to be working in Colombia: Military Professional Resources Inc. (MPRI), Northrop Grumman, Eagle Aviation Services and Technology (EAST), and three helicopter manufacturers – Lockheed Martin, Sikorsky and Bell Textron.

DynCorp, the largest private contractor in Colombia, is said to have employed 335 civilians in the country in 2001, although only one-third were US citizens.[6]

Colombia is reflecting a global trend. According to Peter Singer,[7] an analyst at the Brookings Institution in Washington and author of *Corporate Warriors*, there are currently some 10,000 private military contractors in Iraq; they are performing numerous tasks, including training the new Iraqi military, protecting airports and feeding and housing US troops. This 'privatisation' of the war machine is a recent phenomenon: almost ten times as many private individuals working for contractors were used in the 2003 Iraqi invasion as were used during the 1991 Gulf war. According to Singer, the decision to use more contractors was pragmatic rather than ideological. The Pentagon had very little option, he said, because the military had been downsized and US troops were stretched thin because of their various global commitments. The private contractor industry, worldwide, is believed to have an annual turnover of $100 billion.

There are real advantages to using private contractors. One boon is their greater freedom of action. According to the *Miami Herald*:

> Trying to avoid a direct involvement in Colombia's decades-old war, the Pentagon has forbidden the US military trainers here from entering combat zones or joining police or military operations that could result in clashes with guerrillas or paramilitaries. But no such restrictions apply to the American civilians working for DynCorp or another Virginian firm, Military Professional Resources Inc, known as MPRI, both under contract to help the Colombian security forces.'[8]

This means that the civilians working for the contractors are involved in many operations that are barred to US military personnel. It is members of the unofficial army of private contractors, for instance, who run the Air Bridge Denial

Programme.[9] They fly over the jungle on the look out for suspicious aircraft that could be smuggling cocaine. If their radar locks on to a suspect plane, they attempt radio contact but, if this fails, they can as a last resort shoot down the plane. The programme was abruptly terminated in April 2001, after a plane carrying a US missionary and her baby daughter over the Peruvian jungle was mistakenly shot down. But in August 2003 the programme was quietly restarted, with new safeguards in place. In December 2000 Myles Frechette, former US ambassador to Colombia, told the *St Petersburg Times*: 'It's very handy to have an outfit not part of the US armed forces. Obviously, if someone gets killed or whatever, you can say it's not a member of the armed forces. No one wants to see American military men killed.'[10]

Employing contractors is not a cheap option for the US authorities.

> A State Department internal audit last year [2000] noted that it is much more expensive to rely on contractors instead of Colombians. It said a Dyncorp pilot received $119,305 a year, compared with $45,000 for contractors hired by the Colombian National Police. The State Department also must pay for higher costs for housing and security. Dyncorp has a $200 million, five-year contract with the department, company spokeswomen Janet Wineriter said.[11]

There is no doubt that the high salaries attract the civilian pilots, for they can earn far more than they could hope to be paid for a job in the US.

However, the job is dangerous, as became evident in an incident in February 2003.[12] A single-engined Cessna, loaded with sophisticated photographic equipment, was flying over an isolated jungle region searching for coca plantations, cocaine laboratories and FARC camps. It was providing intelligence for the Colombian armed forces in their counter-narcotics and – less publicly – counter-insurgency operations. The plane crashed and FARC troops killed two members of the crew (a US pilot and a Colombian intelligence officer) and took hostage three other Americans (Marc Gonsalves, Keith Stansell and Thomas Howes), who were working for Northrop Grumman, the huge military contractor.

A few weeks later, on 25 March, another single-engined plane with three civilians on board was sent on a rescue mission to search for the first plane. It also crashed into the jungle, killing all passengers. The families of the dead men discovered that after the first crash Northrop Grunman had created a separate corporation, called CIAO Inc., and switched the men's contracts to this company. The families, who have been told by insurance companies that they do not qualify for the $350,000 death benefit because the men were not working for Northrop Grumman at the time of their death, have started litigation because they believe that the contractor deliberately created the new company 'to protect their profit margin by trying to insulate themselves from liability'.[13] The families are angry, too, at the way the authorities are washing their hands of the incident. 'It's like killing an old stray dog to them, just kick it in the ditch,' said Albert Oliver, whose son Butch was killed in the second crash. 'If they were military, it would be way, way different.'[14] At the time of writing, the three hostages were still being held by the FARC. Their contracts, too, had also been switched to the mysterious CIAO Inc., which had created predictable – and preventable – problems for the men, as the FARC immediately assumed that the company was linked to the CIA.

The incident has provided some insights into the way the contractors work. Butch Oliver and another pilot were hired to replace Paul C. Hooper and Douglas C. Cockes, two pilots who had resigned for safety reasons. In November and December 2002, Hooper and Cockes had written letters to their employer, warning that flying single-engined planes on long missions in remote areas of Colombia was a recipe for disaster.[15] Their letters, first published by the *Los Angeles Times*, suggested that the Cessnas should be replaced with twin-engined Beech King Air 300s. Their suggestion was ignored, so the two pilots resigned. Butch Oliver never had the chance to ease into his new job: shortly after he started work, he was thrown into the desperate search for the survivors of the first crash. 'They were trying to fight a war with makeshift equipment,' said Albert Oliver, a Second World War veteran. 'That's what burns me.' He believes that the contractors were unwilling to switch to twin-engined planes because they did not want to cut into their profit margin (which is said to be 30 or 40%).[16] In all, some 20 people working for private contractors have died in Colombia since 1998.

There have also been reports that some contractors' employees may themselves have been sucked into the lucrative drug trade. According to a Drug Enforcement Agency (DEA) report from 2000,[17] Colombian police officers intercepted a Federal Express package on 12 May 2000, which contained 'two (2) small bottles of a liquid' that 'tested positive for heroin'. The package, which belonged to an unnamed employee of DynCorp, was being sent to the company's headquarters in Florida. The company later alleged that the test had given a 'false positive', but few experts were convinced. Some members of the US Congress are calling for a change in policy. 'Reports that DynCorp employees have been implicated in drug trafficking, the very thing they are paid to help prevent, only strengthens my convictions that outsourcing is the wrong policy,' said Democrat representative, Jan Schakowsky.[18] His advice was ignored by the administration.

DynCorp – poison in Colombia, prisons in Iraq

DynCorp, one of the main companies involved in the spraying of Roundup in Colombia, is a large subcontractor to the British and US armed forces. For years it has been at the spearhead of endeavours by governments in the developed countries to bring private business into the waging of war; it continues to draw all but a tiny percentage of its income from government contracts.

The company was founded in 1946 under the name of California Eastern Airways by a group of Second World War pilots, who thought they could use their military contacts to set up an air cargo business. It prospered during the Korean War, securing most of its contracts from the US government.

The company's activities in Colombia expanded greatly in the 1990s. According to the State Department,[19] DynCorp played a key role in 2001 in the campaign 'to eliminate the cultivation of opium poppy and coca leaf, as well as the trafficking of illicit drugs and their chemical precursors.' In March 2003 this employee-owned business was bought for nearly $1 billion by Computer Sciences Corporation, based in California.

Today DynCorp ranges far and wide outside the US and Colombia. This was exemplified in April 2003 when it was awarded two large contracts, one from the US State Department and another much larger one from the British Ministry of Defence. The US contract was to provide 1,000 staff for US-run prisons in Iraq. The employees had to have 10 years' experience in US police, prisons or courts. At the time the contact was signed, the company said it expected it to bring in $50 million in the first year. Since then, this operation has been shrouded in secrecy. Mike Dickerson, a spokesman for DynCorp's parent company in California, said of its operations in Iraq: 'CSC and its DynCorp International operation are contractually constrained in the extent to which we can publicly comment on the contract,' but his reluctance to talk may have more to do with the murder, torture and humiliation that Iraqi prisoners face in the US-run system that were revealed in 2004. Dickerson denied that his company was involved at the Abu Ghraib prison where prisoners were tortured, killed and photographed by US personnel and contracted civilian staff. [20]

On April 3, 2003, shortly before the Iraq contract was announced, DynCorp International, in a joint venture with another company, was awarded a large contract to manage training ranges for the British Ministry of Defence. The contract, said DynCorp, could be worth more than $948 million over an initial 10-year period and involve 2,000 personnel in 130 sites in Britain. The Blair government was effusive in its praise of DynCorp. Lewis Moonie, at the time the UK junior defence minister, said of the British contract, 'representing best value for money, it will allow us to continue to provide sustainable training for our armed forces.'

A few months earlier, however, officials and politicians had referred in very different terms to DynCorp's practices. On June 22, 2001, in an employment tribunal in Southampton in the UK, Kathryn Bolkovac, a former US policewoman in her forties from Nebraska, who had been recruited by DynCorp for UN service in Bosnia, filed a suit against the company.[21] A mother of three, she had informed her superiors in DynCorp of gross sexual abuse going on among the members of the UN police force, including some people recruited by the company. In a message, sent on October 9, 1999 and produced at the tribunal, Mrs Bolkovac said that women and girls working in Bosnian bars heavily frequented by UN personnel were told by bar owners to perform sex acts. 'The women who refused were locked in rooms and withheld food and outside contact for days or weeks. After this time they are told to dance naked on table tops and sit with clients. If the women still refuse to perform sex acts with the customers, they are beaten and raped in the rooms by the bar owners and their associates. They are told that, if they go to the police, they will be arrested for prostitution and for being an illegal immigrant.'

She was told by DynCorp to stop complaining and was

sacked in April 2001. On November 26, 2002 the chairman of the tribunal, Charles Twiss, said in his judgement: 'It is hard to imagine a case in which a firm has acted in a more callous, spiteful and vindictive manner towards a former employee.' DynCorp was ordered to pay her £110,201 in compensation for her unjustified dismissal. The company said it would appeal against the decision, but in May 2003, as it signed the contract to manage training ranges in Britain, it withdrew its appeal. Using words that seemed to prefigure the subsequent revelations about the torturing and killing of prisoners by the occupation forces in Abu Ghraib and other prisons in Iraq, former Labour defence minister Peter Kilfoyle said: 'I find it difficult to believe that, at a time when bringing law and order to Iraq needs to be handled with delicacy and sensitivity, a private American firm like DynCorp is entrusted with this job.'[22]

Earlier Ben Johnston, an aircraft mechanic who was contracted by DynCorp in 1998 to repair US military helicopters in the Bosnian town of Tuzla, had sued in Fort Worth, alleging that DynCorp dismissed him because he had cooperated with a US Army investigation into allegations that DynCorp employees had illegally purchased weapons and engaged in sexual slavery in Bosnia. The *Washington Post* added that Johnston said his supervisor and several co-workers were regular customers at Bosnian brothels. 'Frustrated that his efforts to stop the illicit trade failed to yield results, he turned to the US Army Criminal Investigation Command, which conducted a sting, obtaining weapons, a pornographic video featuring a DynCorp supervisor, and admission by another employee that he had bought a Romanian woman and an Uzi.' Hours after Bolkovac won her case, lawyers for the company made an undisclosed financial settlement to Johnston.[23]

Notes

1   Juan Ferrero, 'Private US Operatives on Rocky Missions in Colombia', *New York Times*, February 14, 2004.

2   Ken Silverstein, *Private Warriors*, Verso, London, 2001.

3   Remark made by Ken Silverstein, quoted in Jeffrey St. Clair and Alexander Cockburn, 'Ecuadoran Farmers Fight DynCorp's Chemwar on the Amazon', *Counterpunch*, February 27, 2002.

4   St. Clair and Cockburn, op. cit.

5   See, for instance, Juan Ferrero, 'Private US Operatives on Rocky Missions in Colombia', *New York Times*, February 14, 2004.

6   *Los Angeles Times*, August 18, 2001.

7   Quoted by Rachel Van Dongen, 'U.S.'s "private army" grows', *Christian Science Monitor*, September 3, 2003.

8   *Miami Herald*, February 22, 2001.

9   Rachel Van Dongen, op. cit.

10   Quoted in St. Clair and Cockburn, op. cit.

11   Associated Press, May 7, 2001.

12   See Juan Ferrero, op. cit.

13   Bill Torpy, 'Families Want Scrutiny of Drug War in Colombia', *Atlanta Journal–Constitution*, May 9, 2004.

14   Ibid.

15   Juan Ferrero, op. cit.

16   'This World', documentary, BBC 2, December 15, 2004.

17   Quoted in Jason Vest, 'DynCorp's Drug problem', *The Nation*, July 3, 2001.

18   Ibid.

19   Ibid.

20   Dickerson in e-mail to Hugh O'Shaughnessy, May 29, 2004.

21   *Washington Post*, June 23, 2001.

22   *Guardian*, November 29, 2002.

23   *Guardian*, May 3, 2003.

6
Indigenous Peoples Bear the Brunt

The lot of the indigenous groups, traditionally considered to be at the bottom of society in Latin America, has not changed much over the centuries. Some of the atrocities still committed are spine-chilling: Senator Gerardo Jumí, himself an Indian from the Embera community, reported to Rodolfo Stavenhagen of the UN Human Rights Commission that in January 2003 a number of Kogui Indians from the Sierra Nevada de Santa Marta had fallen into the hands of the paramilitaries and, when the their remains were discovered, the fleshy parts of their legs and buttocks were missing: their captors had apparently fried and eaten them.[1] These victims were among some 50 indigenous people in the Sierra Nevada who were killed in 2003. The Office of the UN High Commissioner for Refugees suggests in its report that the cannibalism was carried out by a group from the AUC. The UN report was condemned as one-sided by the Uribe government.

As in the rest of Latin America, the indigenous people of Colombia have died in droves as a result of contact with the outside world: today there are just 1.5 million, compared with almost 10 million at the beginning of the sixteenth century. Divided into 72 different ethnic groups, the Indians account for no more than 0.5% of the population. One of the most baleful chapters in the history of Colombia's indigenous people was written on what are now coca lands. Thousands of indigenous people were enslaved in the Amazon basin and set to work tapping the wild rubber trees to satisfy the burgeoning demand for rubber in Europe (following, first, Faraday's discovery in 1831 of electricity, against which rubber provided insulation, and then, in the 1880s, the invention of the motor car, which required rubber for tyres). News of the rape, murder and torture of Indians reached London, and the Anti-Slavery Society decided to carry out an investigation, putting it into the hands of a Dublin-born Irish official in the British consular service, Roger Casement. He had a distinguished record investigating the rubber trade in equatorial Africa, producing a report that eventually brought about changes in the way the Belgians administered their empire there.

Casement decided to investigate conditions along the Putumayo river. Rising in the lake of La Cocha near Pastos in the south-west of Colombia, the Putumayo river flows east, forming for a long stretch the border with Peru, before eventually flowing into the Amazon river in Brazil. Casement unearthed shocking conditions and calculated that at least 30,000 Indians had died to produce 4,000 tonnes of rubber. He was particularly scathing in his criticisms of one Julio César Araña, who ran a huge rubber empire out of Iquitos through his Peruvian Amazon Company, which was registered in London. The report, published in 1912, unleashed a wave of anger in London, and Casement received a knighthood for his work. Soon the Amazon rubber boom began to collapse (less from moral outrage caused by Casement's findings than as a result of competition from Asian producers who, taking advantage of rubber seedlings smuggled out of the Amazon and nurtured at Kew, set up plantations with much lower production costs). Casement's life ended in tragedy: during the First World War, taking up the cause of Irish independence, he sought German aid for a rebellion but was captured as he landed in Ireland from a German submarine. He was tried and executed in London in 1916 as a traitor. The name of *Cassemeng* still has resonance in Colombia.

As Casement was drawing up his report for the British government, Franciscan Capuchin friars from Catalonia began to take over the missionary work of the Catholic Church in Putumayo.[2] They had their own particular forms of evangelisation. A famous photograph, taken in 1965, summed up the relationship between the friars and their charges. It shows a bearded friar, wearing a Panama hat and sitting on a chair attached to the back of a sweating Indian who, doubled up under the weight, is making his way forward as best he can with the aid of a staff.

Despite the brutal exploitation that Colombia's indigenous people suffered at the hands of Europeans, many indigenous leaders fear that their prospects today are even worse. They believe that one of the aims of Plan Colombia is to drive them off their lands so that powerful economic groups, allied with multinationals, can exploit the economic resources in the subsoil, principally oil and minerals. Colombia, they say, is to be forcibly integrated with the United States through a bilateral trade agreement. 'The primary motivation behind the war is territory,' said Almando Balwena, president of the National Organisation of Indigenous Colombians in April 2003.[3] 'For five centuries we indigenous have maintained our sovereignty and been anti-imperialist. Now Plan Colombia is escalating the war to new levels. The military component of the plan is equivalent to a genocidal war that is intended to eliminate the 72 indigenous cultures from their lands, clearing the way for integration with the United States.'

The Barí

There are many examples of the pressures the indigenous people are facing. The Barí people – whose number has already fallen to the perilously low level of 3,129 – live in a score of villages beside the Catatumbo river in the mountainous jungles in the far north, near the border with Venezuela. 'We fear for our future,' said Jesús Akrokonda, the 42-year-old chief of the Karikachabokira village.[4] The tiny population is seeing its land drenched with poison. The planes fly from an air force base at the town of Tibú, spraying their plantations of maize and yucca. 'The government told us to plant other crops, not coca,' said Jesús, 'but when we did that, their planes came just the same and destroyed our new crops.' The spraying also pollutes the rivers, which provide the Barí with drinking water and where their children learn from an early age to shoot fish with bows and arrows. 'The spraying has a terrible impact on our people,' said Jesús. 'Children are born malformed, with harelips and skin disorders. And respiratory and stomach ailments are common for young and old alike.'

For thousands of years the Barí lived a nomadic life, hunting and fishing in the forests and rivers over which they wandered at will, barefoot and almost naked. But for more than half a century their way of life has been under attack. First, white settlers came to the region and drove them off much of their land. Their nomadic life circumscribed, the Barí were forced to set up permanent villages, weaving simple but elegant houses from the plants of the forest. Then a few decades ago they became enmeshed in Colombia's internal conflict. They were caught in the crossfire between the guerrillas in the mountains and the forces of the state in the valleys where they lived. The bloodshed got even worse when the paramilitaries arrived. At times, Indians died from curable illnesses, such as malaria, because the armed groups would not allow medicines to be brought to them. And now Plan Colombia has reached the Barí, bringing what may prove the kiss of death for this beleaguered community.

The Awá

One dramatic – and emblematic – story of the way in which the 'war on drugs' has affected indigenous groups concerns the 20,000 Awá Indians, who live in the department of Nariño.[5] West of Putumayo, in the canyons cutting into the Andes, where peaks rise 4,250 metres above sea level, lies the city of Pasto, the capital of Nariño. This was once a peaceful area, largely untouched by the conflict. 'It used to be safe to travel through the countryside,' said one indigenous leader. 'We had a way of life that worked well. We had our language, our traditional medicine and a tight social fabric.' The Indians had developed their own system of justice, in which they fined people for fishing or hunting with dynamite (regarded as environmentally unsustainable), wounding someone with a knife, robbing, selling alcoholic spirits or abandoning a wife and children. They were developing an orthography for their language, known as Awapit, with special letters to accommodate some of its very soft consonants.

Plan Colombia changed everything. As spray planes and the US-funded anti-narcotics battalions in the Colombian army fanned through Putumayo's coca fields, the growers – and the armed groups and the narco-traffickers who buy from them – moved westward to Nariño, particularly the coastal zone just west of the town of Ricaurte. People began buying up land, even in the Indian reserves, paying astronomical prices. According to figures from the National Drug Information System, the area under coca cultivation rose from just over 3,000 hectares in 1999 to just over 16,000 hectares in 2002. By 2003 Nariño had replaced Putumayo as the country's chief coca-growing department.[6]

It was a violent shock for the Awá community. Their leaders say that their community had never seen coca until it arrived from Putumayo, as they had not developed a traditional use for it. They admitted, however, that after the coca growers had arrived from Putumayo, some Awá, particularly younger people, planted small quantities of the drug, attracted by the easy money. Along with the coca came violence. The FARC appeared for the first time in 2000, and the AUC was not far behind them. The violence worsened sharply in 2002, as the Uribe government's military offensive in other regions, particularly

Putumayo, pushed larger numbers of FARC guerrillas into this remote area.

Guerrilla groups' and paramilitaries' ruthless competition for drug money and access routes has had a devastating impact on the Awá people, with both forces routinely blockading roads and displacing populations. They have not even respected the Catholic Church. The FARC threatened to kill the bishop of the town of Ipiales if he refused to hand over to them church land which they wanted for coca cultivation.[7] Dozens of indigenous people have been killed, both in selective assassinations and for happening to be in the wrong place at the wrong time. Rape is common. Armed groups routinely steal money, livestock, crops and even clothing. 'You are the owners of this land but we make the rules,' a local FARC leader told an Awá leader.

Alongside the violence is the harm caused by the fumigations. Many of the Indians' crops, including bananas and plantains, maize, yucca, fruit trees, cocoa and medicinal plants, have been destroyed. They are finding it much more difficult to hunt, for birds and game (mainly rabbits and the local species of badger) have been killed or forced to flee deeper into the forest. Domestic animals have perished too, including pigs and thousands of chickens. For the first time the indigenous communities are going hungry. People, particularly toddlers and babies, have been affected with the same ailments, such as fevers and vomiting, that have plagued other communities sprayed with herbicide. The level of tuberculosis is rising. Appeals to the government, the Awá say, have gone unheeded. 'Our former model of society, where food was shared and we bought and sold a few things on the market, has come under attack,' says Gabriel Bisbicús, who heads the Awá People's Indigenous Alliance (UNIPA). 'We can no longer live in the same way as before, when we roamed and hunted freely in the forest. We don't even feel safe on the roads, so it is difficult to sell our produce. We are even scared to travel to towns for medical help when someone is seriously ill.'

The authorities, which for so many decades were entirely absent from the region, have finally appeared, though in many areas it is only the police or the army that the Indians see, for there are few health posts or schools. The authorities have done little to win the trust of the indigenous communities. If an Indian is wearing rubber boots, or carrying a little more money than usual, or fails to produce an identity card (which many Indians do not possess), the military and the police suspect him or her of being a FARC guerrilla or a sympathizer.

The Awá people know that the very survival of their community is at stake. For them, as for all indigenous communities in South America, their territory is sacred. They need to stay on their land, because it enshrines their identity. Bisbicús explained: 'For us, the Awá people, all things that exist – earthquakes, the earth, the trees, the rain, the stones, the wild animals and the spirits – are all Awá people.' Without the natural world they live in, they are nothing.

A much larger community than the Barí, the Awá are beginning to organise effectively. Bisbicús is part of a small team with an office in the departmental capital of Pastos. They have bought a mobile phone and a computer, have set up their own website,[8] and have printed calendars and other literature about their plight for national distribution. They are meticulously gathering all the evidence they can lay their hands on to record the impact of the fumigations on their reserves, which vary in size from 50 to 17,000 hectares and altogether cover 342,561 hectares. They have maps and detailed records of the sprayings in all the reserves. To take a typical case, the reserve at Honda Río Guiza, they have records that show that the 60 families living in this reserve have 200 hectares of land under cultivation and another 180 hectares of virgin forest, that it has been sprayed three times and has suffered damage to plantains, yucca and maize, and that the community has received no compensation from the Colombian or US governments nor indeed any help of any kind. As this book went to press, the spraying was still going on, and planes with their escorts of armed helicopters still buzzed over their lands.

Indigenous peoples fight back

Indigenous communities have suffered more than most. Because the Indians inhabit isolated regions, their lands have tended to come under the influence of insurgent groups, particularly the guerrillas. For decades they coexisted in relative tranquillity with the insurgents, but then the official armed forces and the paramilitaries took the conflict deeper into the countryside. The conflict was more intense in regions with rich natural resources, particularly oil, or with plentiful coca plantations. Whole indigenous communities were caught in the crossfire.

In the early days the Indians' resistance tended to be isolated and fragmentary. In 1971, however, communities began for the first time to work together to organise their struggle to get official recognition of their ownership rights and to win back some of the land they had lost. They made real advances: the new constitution in 1991 recognised for the first time that indigenous authorities had jurisdiction over their ancestral lands. But these very achievements meant that the indigenous communities represented more of a threat to those groups that were trying to drive them off their lands. 'The landowners started organising their own militias to force us off the land,' said Feliciano Valencia, an indigenous leader.[9] 'When these groups couldn't drive us out, they called in the police and the army. Since 1971, 980 Indians have been killed in the struggle to recover our land.'

Some communities have become disheartened. In early 2004 the United Nation High Commissioner for Refugees began a project with shamans in various indigenous communities to see if anything could be done to halt a spate of suicides among young Indians who were losing the will to live.

Other communities have started using their own system of indigenous justice to bring charges against those who have violated their rights. In February 2004 16 indigenous leaders in the department of Cauca ordered Colonel Juan Vicente Trujillo of the army's Pichincha battalion and soldiers under his command to appear at their court to answer the charge of shooting dead the Indian Olmedo Ul at an army roadblock on December 31, 2003. This was the first time an indigenous group had used its own courts against a member of the armed forces, although they had brought similar charges against members of the FARC and ELN, who were similarly accused of murdering Indians. On the day scheduled for the trial some 3,000 Indians gathered in the village of Bodega Alta. When (as expected) the colonel failed to appear, Armando Valbuena, a Guayú Indian, and two members of the Paez indigenous community, sitting under a mango tree, tried the colonel *in absentia*.

Indigenous communities are also staging massive demonstrations against the way they are being treated. In September 2004 some 70,000 Indians took part in a 4-day march to Cali, the capital of the department of Cauca. The march, organised 'to defend life, justice, happiness, freedom and autonomy', is believed to have been the largest indigenous demonstration in the history of Colombia. Seven indigenous communities in Cauca organised the event, which they called a *minga*, an indigenous word for the ancestral practice of communal work for a common goal. Indians from other regions, along with Afro-Colombians and peasant families, also took part. Several commentators pointed out that the indigenous people were the only sector capable of organising such a large protest.

President Uribe was critical of the march, accusing it of having a hidden political agenda. 'Tell the truth, admit that you are a political party, and you want to march and protest,' he said.[10] The indigenous communities responded with a communiqué in which they said:

Of course, our *minga* is Political with a capital P, because defending indigenous and collective rights is Political; rejecting the dismantling of the social structures of the democratic state is Political; defending indigenous lands and their autonomous government is Political; opposing the free trade agreement [with the United States] is Political; rejecting the murders, forced disappearances, forced displacement, violence and war is Political …

The Indians made it clear that they had not expected a favourable reaction from the government. 'We do not speak for the government to hear,' the communiqué stated. 'We talk to the people.' Well aware of the need to create their own communication systems to publicise their message, they deployed a number of 'community communicators', who operate small mobile radio stations.[11] One of these communicators, whose photograph appeared in many Colombian newspapers, was powering a transmitter on a specially adapted tandem bicycle.

Notes

1   Reported in *El Tiempo*, March 11, 2004.
2   See Víctor Daniel Bonilla, *Siervos de Dios y Amos de Indios*, Bogotá, 1968, and *Servants of God or Masters of Men*, Penguin, London, 1972.
3   *Washington Free Press*, April 13, 2003.
4   Personal interview with Hugh O'Shaughnessy, February 2004.
5   This account relies heavily on a report posted on the internet by a US human rights activist, Adam Isacson.
6   United Nations Office on Drugs and Crime, *Colombia Coca Survey for 2003*, Bogotá, June 2004.
7   Consultoría para los Derechos Humanos y el Desplazamiento, *Plan Colombia: Contraproductos y crisis humanitaria. Fumigaciones y desplazamiento en la frontera con Ecuador*, Bogotá, October 29, 2003.
8   www.Awaunipa.org
9   Constanza Viera, 'Indigenous March for Peace', IPS news, September 20, 2004.
10 Ibid.
11 Phillip Cryan, 'Indigenous Mobilisation in Colombia – Speaking Truth to People, not Power', *CounterPunch*, Petrolia, Calif., October 2, 2004.

Conclusion: Rethinking the Strategy

Even in Uribe's Colombia there are influential people who are calling for a scrapping of the present strategy. One of the most powerful is Lucho Garzón, a left-wing politician who was elected mayor of Bogotá in 2003. He is campaigning for an immediate halt to spraying as part of a broad rejection of what he calls 'the failed prohibitionist strategy against drugs'. Instead, he is suggesting that farmers be encouraged gradually to give up the cultivation of coca, with the introduction of 'focused investment' in the land. He is calling for a new international strategy in which the burden of phasing out drugs will be taken away from the weakest link in the chain – the peasants of Colombia and other Andean countries. His view, that people in the producing countries are being forced by the richer consuming countries to bear an excessively large share of the costs of drug eradication, is widely shared in Colombia. He proposes a shift in counter-narcotics policy from repression of drugs to the treatment of addicts. Why is it, he asks, that the phasing out of tobacco in the US has been generally successful while the phasing out of drugs has failed? He suggests that an international conference be called to review international drug policies and to look for alternatives.

Garzón's argument coincides with a worldwide shift in attitudes. The world is beginning to reject the way drug misuse is routinely depicted as one of the greatest evils confronting humanity that can be tackled only with 'zero tolerance' policies, while alcohol and smoking are not criminalized but regarded as issues of personal choice. Yet drinking and smoking do far greater damage to health. The leading causes of death in the US in 2000 were: tobacco (435,000 deaths, 18.1% of the total), poor diet and physical inactivity (400,000, 16.6%) and alcohol consumption (85,000, 3.5%). The illicit use of drugs was much lower in the list (17,000 deaths, 0.7%).[1] The lobbies mounted by the alcohol and tobacco industries and the dependence of many governments on the revenues brought in by taxes on drinking and smoking undoubtedly help to explain this paradox.

The particular strength of the tobacco lobby was neatly summed up by Martin Jelsma and Pien Metaal of the Trans-national Institute in Amsterdam: 'For example, the fact that that the European Union spends more every single year in subsidies to European tobacco farmers – around $1 billion – than the combined sum the whole world has allocated to alternative development efforts for coca and opium poppy farmers all through the past decades, remains a sorry example of policy priorities that are out of balance.'[2]

It is becoming increasingly evident that coercion is failing to stem either drug trafficking or the consumption of illicit drugs. In 2002 the Home Affairs Committee of the British House of Commons produced a gloomy report about official drug strategies in the UK. Chris Mullin MP, its chairman, commented:

> If there is any single lesson from the experience of the last 30 years, it is that that policies based wholly or mainly on enforcement are destined to fail. It remains an unhappy fact that the best efforts of police and Customs have had little, if any, impact on the availability of illegal drugs and this is reflected in the prices on the street, which are as low now as they have ever been.[3]

In evidence to the Committee, Francis Wilkinson, the recently retired Chief Constable of the police force of Gwent in Wales, made the following comment about the British drug strategy: 'There was not a single year in the 1990s when one could be hopeful about the progress of the drugs problem in this country. I see absolutely no rational basis for thinking that might be different in the next three years.'[4] Moreover, much of the violence generated by drugs stems from its illegality. All over the world, rival trafficking groups wage vicious wars for control of the lucrative networks and, once addicted to drugs, individuals get involved in crime to feed their expensive habit. According to the US Department of Justice, about a quarter of drug addicts in the US commit crimes to raise money for their drugs.[5]

As a result, the list of countries that are moving away from a strategy of blind bellicosity towards drugs is long and growing. In Switzerland and the Netherlands the emphasis is shifting away from law enforcement towards regulation and harm reduction. There have been calls in the Jamaican parliament for the decriminalisation of ganja (marijuana). At the end of February 2004 the Basque government in Spain announced that, in the light of successful experiments in Andalusia and Catalonia, it was ready to supply heroin on prescription to addicts whenever the central government authorised such a policy.

Against this background the actions undertaken by the US government are increasingly being seen by the international community as unreasonable, unscientific and bullying. Many observers are beginning to say that it makes no sense to spray poison over the land of a large South American country, damaging human health and destroying plants, animals and the environment. Although the fumigation may lead to a temporary dip in coca cultivation, it will not permanently disrupt the flow of drugs and may actually lead to an increase in coca production, as peasant families, with their livelihoods destroyed, move into remote areas and turn to coca and poppies as the only profitable crops.

The counter-offensive is slowly gaining momentum as knowledge of the extent of the damage being done in Colombia is seeping into the public domain, despite the best efforts of the

Colombian and US governments to suppress the evidence. The influential Washington Office on Latin America (WOLA) published in early 2005 a comprehensive study of US drug policy in Latin America. It observed that the situation was growing worse year by year:

> Illicit drug use, once considered a problem of the global north, is now rampant across the region. A particularly adverse effect is that those who get involved in local drug-trafficking networks are often paid in drugs rather than cash. They in turn sell the drugs on local streets, stimulating new markets and illicit drug consumption.

Moreover, the study concluded that, far from ameliorating the situation, US drug policy was actually weakening the social fabric of many Latin American countries:

> Our study points to serious concerns with regard to the many ways in which U.S. international drug control policy is undermining democracy and democratic development. These areas of concern include: the expansion of the role of military forces in drug control efforts; inappropriate roles assigned to police forces; human rights violations; restrictions on civil liberties; the fostering of political instability; undermining local decision-making; lack of transparency and accountability; and abuses resulting from forced eradication of crops used in drug production.

Although the study does not go as far as to call for the decriminalisation of drugs, it says that the US government should recognise that interdiction alone will not work. Instead of concentrating on repression, the US authorities should be encouraging debate on alternatives: 'Across the Western Hemisphere, civil society groups, local politicians, the media and the public at large should be encouraged to participate in a meaningful debate on how to best approach the very real problems of illicit drug production, trafficking and consumption, and the violence they generate.' And, the study says, the US authorities should be paying far more attention to the demand-side of the equation:

> Drug policy goals should be recast in public health terms and seek to reduce the harm caused by illicit drugs. This approach implies reorienting strategies to focus on developing effective treatment and education programs, including treatment upon demand, HIV/AIDS programs, realistic prevention strategies and community development.

Several respected institutions go further. In Britain the conservative weekly *The Economist* has for years called for illicit drugs to be legalised. The equally conservative Hoover Institution at Stanford University in the US reached a similar conclusion in a paper it published a paper in 2001: 'Colombia's crisis, and the crises in varying stages in neighbouring countries, cannot be squarely tackled until the enormous financial incentives and thus profits of the illegal drug trade are eliminated. This would require a decriminalisation of consumption in the user countries.'[6]

This gradual shift in perceptions of the 'war on drugs' is to be welcomed, but to some extent it misses the point about US involvement in Colombia. As we have noted throughout this book, the US government has used the 'war on drugs' as a smokescreen behind which it has ruthlessly pursued the broader goal of defending its strategic interests in the region. As was evident from the testimony given to Congress by General Peter Pace, Commander-in-Chief of SouthCom, quoted at length in chapter three, the reason the Pentagon seeks to maintain geopolitical stability in Latin America is to allow US companies 'unhindered access' to strategic natural resources and to Latin America's markets. In Colombia, this means defeating the guerrillas, opening new areas of oil and mineral resources for US investment, and integrating Colombia more closely within the US economic empire. As a result, the Pentagon will assess its policies by their success, not only in combating drugs, but also in contributing to these broader goals. This means that policies which from a strictly counter-narcotics perspective may appear misguided may in fact be considered partially successful from the Pentagon's viewpoint.

For instance, the Washington Office on Latin America study upbraids the US government for pursuing drug control policies that have dealt with the problem in almost exclusively military terms: 'U.S. drug control policies have contributed to confusing military and law enforcement functions, militarising local police forces, and bringing the military into a domestic law enforcement role. They have thus strengthened military forces at the expense of civilian authorities.'[7] The Pentagon, however, may well consider it beneficial for the US's long-term strategic interests for Latin American armed forces (over which the Pentagon has considerable influence) to increase their strength vis-à-vis the civilian authorities. It is, of course, debatable whether or not the Pentagon is right in this assessment: this then becomes a debate not over the Pentagon's perceived foolishness in pursuing ill-conceived drug policies but over the much broader question of what kind of relationship the US authorities, both civilian and military, should forge with its southern neighbours.

In the 1970s and 1980s the US military held great sway over Latin America by training the local armed forces in the 'doctrine of national security' and by getting them not only to fight dirty wars to 'defeat communism' but also to overthrow democratically elected governments regarded as politically suspect by Washington. With the collapse of communism, the Pentagon ran the risk of not having any justification for its heavy involvement in Latin America. The 'war on drugs' emerged in the nick of time to provide it with a new pretext. As the WOLA study confirms, this has allowed the US authorities to carry on having a large say in issues that should be decided by democratically elected, national governments:

Responsibility for the design, implementation and oversight of drug policy should lie with civilian authorities in each country. Yet off the record officials in such countries as Peru, Bolivia and Ecuador complain that local counter-drug forces report first to the U.S. embassy and that civilian authorities are often kept out of the loop. Moreover, military and police forces often negotiate directly with Washington on aid and training packages with little civilian government input.[8]

The tale was given a new twist by 9/11. Whereas in the past the US authorities had to maintain the pretext at least of intervening only in those areas of policy-making concerned with the 'war on drugs', they are now waging a 'war on terror', which gives them a reason to interfere in a much broader range of issues. So far, this has not had a great impact on US relations with Latin America because Washington's interest has been focused almost exclusively on the Middle East, but this seems certain to change in the future.

One country that is likely to be targeted is Colombia's unruly neighbour to the east, Venezuela. Venezuela is of greater importance to US strategic interests than Colombia: it is the fifth largest exporter of crude oil in the world and the fourth most important supplier to the US. Yet under Hugo Chávez Venezuela has displayed a worrying independence of mind, playing an active role in OPEC and forging close links with Cuba and, more recently, China. Unless events in the Middle East spiral completely out of control, the US government will be anxious in one way or another to neutralise Chávez in the near future. Colombia, which is being groomed as the US's staunchest ally in a troubled region, will undoubtedly be expected to play a key role in the upcoming offensive against Chávez.

It is clear that Colombia is, for Washington, a key pawn in the South American context. The US decision to introduce chemical warfare in Colombia may thus have more in common with the Vietnam War than is generally appreciated. Just as in

Vietnam, the US is resorting to chemical weapons, with no regard for the cost to human beings and to the environment, in order to defend its geopolitical goals in a crucial region. The strategy failed in Vietnam because of the courageous resistance of millions of ordinary people, both in Vietnam itself and on the streets of US and European cities. It is likely that in Colombia too a fundamental reversal in US policy will be achieved only by dual action: a decision by the Colombian people to elect to power a politician who is opposed to the economic and political take-over of their country; and mass-based protests in both Colombia and the industrialised countries against the way Washington is inflicting misery on thousands of poor Colombians through its use of chemical warfare in pursuit of its own economic, political and military objectives.

Notes

1   Ali H. Mokdad, PhD, James S. Marks, MD, MPH, Donna F. Stroup, PhD, MSc, Julie L. Gerberding, MD, MPH, 'Actual Causes of Death in the United States, 2000,' *Journal of the American Medical Association*, vol. 291, no. 10, March 10, 2004, pp. 1238, 1241.
2   Washington Office on Latin America, *Cracks in the Vienna Consensus: The UN Drug Control Debate*, January 2004.
3   House of Commons Home Affairs Committee, op.cit.
4   Ibid.
5   Bureau of Justice Statistics, *Drug Use and Crime*, U.S. Department of Justice Statistics, http://www.ojp.usdoj.gov/bjs/welcome.html
6   War and Lack of Governance in Colombia: Narcos, Guerrillas, and U.S. Policy by Edgardo Buscaglia and William Ratliff.
7   Washington Office on Latin America, op. cit.
8   Ibid.

Index